MONASTIC
GARDENS

MONASTIC GARDENS

✛

MICK HALES

STEWART, TABORI & CHANG

NEW YORK

Published in 2000 by
Stewart, Tabori & Chang
A division of U.S. Media Holdings, Inc.
115 West 18th Street
New York, NY 10011

Distributed in Canada by
General Publishing Company Ltd.
30 Lesmill Road
Don Mills, Ontario, Canada M3B 2T6

Library of Congress
Cataloging-in-Publication Data
Hales, Michael.
Monastic gardens / by Mick Hales.
         p. cm.
Includes bibliographical references (p.)
and index.
ISBN 1-55670-982-X
1. Monastery gardens—United States.
2. Monastery gardens—Great Britain. 3.
Monastery gardens—France. 4.
Monastery gardens—United States—
Pictorial works. 5. Monastery gar-
dens—Great Britain—Pictorial works.
6. Monastery gardens—France—
Pictorial works. I. Title.
SB457.35.H35   2000
712'.7'0222—dc21   00-022478

Printed in Great Britain

10 9 8 7 6 5 4 3 2 1

First Printing

PAGE 1:
*Purple petunias in a
carved stone planter in
the formal garden of
Saint Martin Abbey,
Liguge, France.*

FRONTISPIECE:
*Sunrise at Saint Martin
Abbey, Liguge, France.*

PAGE 8:
*The Virgin Mary and
Holy Child statue in
the southeast corner of
the cloister walkway at
Notre Dame Abbey, Le
Bec Hellouin, France.*

To my beautiful wife, Christine,
who accompanied me on much of this journey with support
and constant encouragement, and to our family,
Mark, Micah, and August.

ACKNOWLEDGMENTS

My especial thanks to Brother William Brown, Holy Cross Monastery; Brother Victor Antoine, Our Lady of the Resurrection; Sister Penelope Mary, Community of the Holy Spirit; Brother Anthony Hare, Burford Priory; and Susan Taylor Moody, The Cloisters, Metropolitan Museum of Art.

Thanks to all the abbots and abbesses who allowed their gardens to be photographed, some for the first time. Thanks also to the monks and nuns who shared their experiences and beliefs, including Dame Gertrude Brown, Stanbrook Abbey; Mother Rosemary, Convent of the Incarnation; Sister Mary John, Saint Mary's Abbey; Sister Jane Mary, Burnham Abbey; Brother Daniel Rees, Downside Abbey; Mother Gillian, Tymawr Convent; Brother Benedict, Holy Cross Abbey; Mother Madeleine Mary, Saint Hilda's House; Brother Jason, Little Portion Friary; Father Guerric, Mepkin Abbey; Brother Harold Thibodeau, Abbey of Gethsemani; Mother Felicitas and Mother Hildegard, Our Lady of the Rock; Mother Placid and Mother Margaret Georgina, Abbey of Regina Laudis; Brother Christopher O'Brian, Saint Joseph's Abbey; Brother Robert Halger, Mount Calvary; Sister Yolande and Sister Myriam, Notre Dame des Gardes Abbey; Father Michael Bozell, Saint-Pierre Abbey; Sister Sonia Duthoit, Sainte Scholastique Abbey; Father Luc, Abbey of Fleury; Father Vincent Desprez, Saint Martin Abbey; Brother Jean Marie, Notre Dame du Bec Abbey; and Brother Laurent, Abbey of En Calcat. Also, my thanks to Esther De Waal.

† TABLE OF

Contents

MONASTERIES VISITED AND PHOTOGRAPHED FOR THIS BOOK

UNITED STATES

The Abbey of Gethsemani, Kentucky

The Abbey of Regina Laudis, Connecticut

Holy Cross Abbey, Virginia

Holy Cross Monastery, New York

Little Portion Friary, New York

Mepkin Abbey, South Carolina

Monastery of Our Lady of the Resurrection, New York

Monastery of Our Lady of the Rock, Washington

Mount Calvary Monastery, California

St. Joseph's Abbey, Massachusetts

ENGLAND AND WALES

Burford Priory, Oxon

Burnham Abbey, Berkshire

Convent of the Incarnation, Fairacres, Oxfordshire

Downside Abbey, Stratton-on-the-Fosse, Somerset

Saint Mary's Abbey, West Malling, Kent

Stanbrook Abbey, Worcester

Tymawr Convent, Gwent

FRANCE

Abbey of Bellefontaine, Begrolles-En-Mauges

Abbey of En Calcat, Dourgne

Abbey of Fleury, Saint-Benoit-sur-Loire

The Abbey of Mont Saint Michel, Mont Saint Michel

Notre Dame Abbey, Le Bec Hellouin

Notre Dame des Gardes Abbey, St.-George des Gardes

Saint Martin Abbey, Liguge

The Abbey of Sainte-Croix, Poitiers

Sainte Scholastique Abbey, Dourgne

Saint-Pierre Abbey, Solesmes

Sainte-Cécile Abbey, Solesmes

The paradigm that monasteries are austere and frightening places comes mostly from ignorance, but it is understandable how that image developed. Adorned with "Private" and "Keep Out" signs, high walls, and long driveways, monasteries reveal little of their grounds and inhabitants. Only chiming chapel bells and trees protruding over the wall give a hint to what lies within, leaving much to the imagination of outsiders. Ultimately the message is clear—whoever lives in this mysterious place wishes to be left alone.

I am grateful I now know how wrong that image is, but still whenever I ring the door bell of a monastery, there seems to be an interminable wait as old fears return. Who am I to be disturbing the silence? Am I dressed correctly? Does anyone really live here? Did the bell work? Finally, the heavy door opens. Immediately, I am struck by how happy the greeter is. The sheer happiness monks and nuns enjoy is irrepressible; it seems to pour out of them. The skeptic might say it's because they are expected to greet all people as though Jesus were knocking on their door. But, even at monasteries that are literally overwhelmed by visitors, the monks and nuns radiate an intrinsic happiness that most of us would envy.

They are living in a private world of prayer, community, stability, and enclosure. Guided by ancient rules, interpreted by the abbot or abbess, the communities steer their way through the modern world very carefully. Holding tightly to aspects of the past they revere, while at the same time accepting new tools of modern life, if appropriate, they move forward with their faith.

One of the foundations of Christian monastic life throughout its seventeen hundred years has been a close, spiritual relationship with gardens and gardening. As a nun in England explained it to me:

We are striving for humility in our lives, to draw closer to our God. It is not an accident that the humus, or the soil, comes from the same word. It's the base from which everything grows. Gardening and my spiritual life go together.

From the beginning gardening was a part of Christian monasticism. St. Anthony, reported to be the first Christian monk (270-350), gave up all his property and became a hermit—and a gardener—in the Egyptian desert. His friend, St. Hilarion, noted that, "these vines and these little trees did he plant; the pool did he contrive, with much laboring for the watering of his garden; with his rake did he break up the earth for many years."

The third century Christian, St. Phocas, is reported to have lived by the Black Sea and ardently kept a garden. He welcomed two strangers, and as it turned out, they were soldiers sent to find and persecute him. On learning this he went into his garden and dug a grave. He then identified himself to the soldiers as the object of their search, where upon they beheaded him and buried him in the grave he had prepared within his garden.

In the seventh century, St. Fiacre is said to have had a garden in the woods near Meaux, France, so revered that the wild animals of the forest would not enter and eat from it. It was as if his unwalled garden was spiritually enclosed.

In these brief examples of early Christian gardeners, some of the important characteristics of the relationship of the monastic life and gardening have emerged. The essence of this book is how these simple aspects of gardening are symbolic of life itself: the planting, the heavy labor, the tools, the breaking up, tending and love of soil, water in the garden, burial in the garden, a reverence for flowers as part God's creation, and finally the importance of an enclosure and gardening year after year in the same place.

Many of these features are common to gardens outside of religious communities, but what makes monastery gardens so different and, as time progresses, so special, is that the monks or nuns still toil at their main work in life—prayer—while gardening. Prayer is the primary work of those following a monastic life, and is undertaken not only in the frequent offices of the church, but constantly, with every possible moment. This has a very powerful way of focusing the mind, of seeing God in everything and everyone. The monk whose life is set in the rhythm of liturgical and seasonal cycles, whose mind is focused on spiritual thoughts and whose body is actively gardening, is well equipped to grapple with the questions of life. The Bible has numerous passages which interpret spiritual direction through horticultural explanations, suggesting that this relationship of spiritual focus and activity with the soil was intended.

As our society continues to speed up with mechanization and technology it is easy for us to be removed from tending the soil. I believe we miss out on many of the gifts we were intended to receive, when there is no time or desire to work with the soil. Just as monasteries were the arks of learning in the early Middle Ages, as the twenty-first century dawns, they can share with us their knowledge of the value of gardening for physical and mental health, and our stewardship of the earth.

What is a monastery garden? Usually there are several different gardens within the walls of a monastery or directly associated with them. All of the monks' outside needs have to be met in the grounds of the monastery. As Brother Vincent of Liguge, France, replied:

It is a grace. It is a grace from God that we have our garden. We do not have a High Street we can step out into. All of our needs must be taken care of in this space.

By looking at these different gardens and what roles they perform, a larger story unfolds. The cloister garth is at the very heart of the monastery, and beyond that lies the sacristan's or cutting garden for flower offerings in the church, the physic or herb garden for health, an orchard, a vegetable and soft fruit garden, and a burial garden for monks who have left the physical body.

Gardens are living entities and quickly reflect the care or neglect they receive. Not all the inhabitants of a community are involved with the garden directly as gardeners, but certainly they all use them and appreciate them. Even the infirm and elderly are helped by younger members to get into the garden regularly. The monks and nuns were generous and trusting enough to open their enclosures to me and my wife, Christine; they shared what their gardens meant to them, and were always full of life. I am very grateful for their generosity and hopeful that some of their spirit of happiness and a small portion of their quiet knowledge will be communicated through this book.

I

THE CLOISTER GARTH

A PLACE OF SIMPLICITY THAT BELIES ITS DEEP POWER, THE CLOISTER GARTH, OR GARDEN, HAS MANY PRACTICAL AS WELL AS SYMBOLIC COMPONENTS. THE BASIC COURTYARD DESIGN THAT CHRISTIAN MONAS-TERIES HAVE ADAPTED FOR THEIR USE IS THOUGHT TO HAVE ITS ORIGINS IN ROMAN COUNTRY HOUSES. BY BUILDING THE HOUSE AND FARM BUILDINGS AROUND A CENTRAL YARD, THE ROMANS CREATED AN ENCLOSURE THAT SHELTERED THE ANIMALS AND PROTECTED EVERYONE FROM THE ELEMENTS. IN FACT THE LATIN WORD *CLAUSTRIUM*, ROOT OF THE WORD "CLOISTER," MEANS "SHUT-IN PLACE."

PRECEDING PAGES:
Sunlight pours into the corridor of the cloister garth at Saint Martin Abbey, Liguge, France.

OPPOSITE:
Formal topiary resembling a fleur-de-lis in one of two cloister garths at Saint-Pierre Abbey, Solesmes, France.

CENTERED AT THE **HEART** OF THE COMMUNITY, THE

AND **SAFETY** WHILE ACTING AS

There is typically a lean-to canopy roof running around the perimeter of the garden, creating a covered walkway with a fixed wall on the outside and pillared supports on the inside. This design combines protection from the elements with exposure to fresh air, green grass, and the constant movement of daylight. Centered at the heart of the community, the cloister garth provides a sense of privacy and safety while acting as a connecting passage between the chapel, refectory, dormitory, and library. This combination of elements is known as the claustral range. It may not be the only route from one place to the next within the monastery, but its qualities are very inviting.

On entering the cloister from the darkness of the buildings the green garden is partially hidden by the piers of the arches. Drawn forward in search of a better view, the visitor finds that every time he approaches a point where he expects to see the whole garden, another column obstructs his view. The only way to see it in its entirety is to move from the protection of the walkway into the garden proper, but this is like crossing an invisible line: the rich green seems to be bounded by an imaginary fence, as if to keep us from walking into the garden. Although in reality there is no prohibition against stepping into the center of the garth, it is easy to feel as if we have broken an unspoken rule. Viewed from the center, the garth fails to cast its spell: the spatial qualities break down when the visual tension between the walkway's arches and the garden disappears. The monks are well aware of this: as a brother from the Abbey of En Calcat has observed,

TOP:
Mother Placid in the garden of The Abbey of Regina Laudis, Connecticut.

ABOVE AND LEFT:
Details of cloisters at Notre Dame Abbey, Le Bec Hellouin, France, and Saint-Pierre Abbey, Solesmes, France.

CLOISTER GARTH PROVIDES A SENSE OF **PRĪVACY**

A **CONNECTING PASSAGE...**

TOP AND RIGHT:
Details of cloisters at
Abbey of En Calcat,
Dourgne, France, and
Saint Martin Abbey,
Ligugé, France.

although they are constantly walking around the garden or sitting along its perimeter, the only time the monks actually enter is to tend the plants.

Along with the feeling of trespassing, standing in the center of a cloister garth can give one the sense of being in a fish bowl. The garden at Stanbrook Abbey in England, for instance, is surrounded on three sides by a tall brick Victorian building with a great many gothic windows, all facing the garden. It is difficult not to lose one's sense of security when venturing into the middle from the perimeter walkway.

Walking the perimeter of a cloister garth is like exploring a labyrinth or medieval garden maze: just when you think you have arrived, you find you need to look further. This experience of being pulled forward can awaken the realization that what really matters in life is the journey or search for meaning, rather than the expectation that meaning will be suddenly revealed in a single, exceptional moment.

The sense of continuity is heightened by the purity and simplicity of the plants typically found in cloister gardens, which tend to be green: grass, simple boxwood forms, some shrubbery and evergreen trees. The layout is formal, divided into four parts around a central ornamental element. Wherever possible this includes water, usually in the form of a pool or a fountain. A glance at Genesis 2:8, (the first book of the Bible), reminds us of God's connection to gardens, and the symbolism of water in the garden of Eden:

> *Now the Lord God had planted a garden in the east, in Eden; and there he put the man he had formed. And the Lord God*

made all kinds of trees grow out of the ground—trees that were pleasing to the eye and good for food. In the middle of the garden were the tree of life and the tree of the knowledge of good and evil. A river watering the garden flowed from Eden; from there it was separated into four headwaters.

The passage also reveals the symbolism behind the garden's division into four parts by paths of brick, cobbled pebbles, or gravel. Similarly, trees planted in the cloister represent the tree of life.

Christians believe that God lightens our darkness: the cloister garden, which is open to the heavens, serves as a reminder of this to the monks, by funneling daylight into the center of the monastery. Often, members of a community like to sit in the cloister at twilight, reading by the last rays of light before Compline, the evening service. Modern science supports the importance of daylight in our emotional health through studies of Sensory Affect Disorder, a form of depression caused by insufficient sunlight during the winter months. Writing over a hundred years ago, Florence Nightingale acknowledged the role of daylight in promoting recovery from illness:

Second only to fresh air, I should be inclined to rank light in importance for the sick. Direct sunlight, not only daylight, is necessary for speedy recovery...

I mention from experience, as quite perceptible in promoting recovery, the being able to see out the window, instead of looking against a dead wall; the bright

OPPOSITE:
The central pond of the cloister garth at Stanbrook Abbey, Worcester, England.

colors of flowers; the being able to read by the light of the window close to the head. It is generally said the effect is upon the mind. Perhaps so, but it is not less so upon the body on that account.

Like daylight, the color green, even glimpsed momentarily, can have an uplifting effect. The setting of green grass within the cloister range has long been known to have a unique power and grace and to exert a kind of subliminal attraction. As early as the twelfth century, Saint Hildegard of Bingen gave a new meaning to the Latin word *viriditas* ("greenness") to describe the calming and healing power that she recognized in the color green: she called it "greening power" and likened its rejuvenating spiritual effect to the power of creativity:

> *... greening love hastens to the aid of all. With the passion of heavenly yearning, people who breathe this dew produce rich fruit.*

In effect the green of the cloister

RIGHT:
*Stone carving of Mary
and crucified Jesus beside
a pathway in the garden
of Saint Mary's Abbey,
West Malling, Kent,
England.*

BELOW:
*The cloister garth at
Saint-Pierre Abbey,
Solesmes, France, is
centered in the claustral
range with a corridor to
the formal French garden.*

garth works like an oasis in the desert: it is a place for restoring oneself, a place of serenity that pulls one in. Even if there is only enough time to pass quickly by, the sight of this green is invigorating.

Living in a building with good light is mentally uplifting, but it has other qualities as well. One of these is timekeeping. It may strike outsiders as incongruous but daily life within a monastery is fully scheduled, between the divine offices, meal times and many other commitments. Tardiness was enough of a serious offense to warrant a separate chapter in St. Benedict's Rule. Titled "Latecomers to the Work of God [i.e., communal prayer] or to Meals," it specifies:

> *As soon as the signal for Divine Office is heard, the brethren must leave whatever they have been engaged in doing, and hasten with all speed, but with dignity, so that foolishness finds no stimulus. Nothing, therefore, is to be given preference over the work of God.*

Visitors to monasteries find that they, too, are expected to keep their appointments to the minute. The cloister garth becomes a useful timepiece: the shadows cast by the walkway columns work like the hands of an enormous sundial, telling the time with considerable accuracy for those who frequently circumnavigate this central chimney of light during the course of the day.

Timekeeping enables punctuality, which enhances the rhythm of the monk's routine and contributes to the stability of the community as a whole.

Stability is one of the principal differences between monastic and secular life: where people living in the world move frequently to pursue careers, attend school, visit family, or simply find a better climate, monasteries stay in the same place, and the members of their community stay there with them. The high degree of permanence and stability offers the cloistered religious a special kind of security and the surroundings that encourage living a spiritual life.

Another special use of the cloister is the processional. Dating back possibly

OPPOSITE:
A second cloister garth at Saint-Pierre Abbey, Solesmes, France, has a classic configuration with a central water feature and four pathways dividing the garden, surrounded by cypresses.

RIGHT:
The hills of Santa Barbara, California, form a backdrop to the perennial cloister garden at Mount Calvary Monastery.

monastery is rooted in French culture and that it is part of the local community, not isolated from it. The second cloister is a green garden with four cypresses surrounding the small pool at the center. As is often the case with monasteries, the various buildings of Solesmes are in different architectural styles, reflecting the historical periods in which they were built. Naturally this variety affects the cloister, as it is largely defined by the buildings around it. The architecture at Solesmes, for instance, is strongly influenced by modern interpretations of the Alhambra. The cloister at Saint Mary's Abbey in West Malling,

England, is quite different; consisting of simple pebble work and a central fountain, it is plain but remarkably powerful, with an almost Japanese feeling. Here building styles range from a cloister walk dating to the year 1220 to the new chapel, built in 1966.

At the especially welcoming Notre Dame des Gardes Abbey in St.-George des Gardes, France, the nuns have rejected the formal style and instead made a garden of randomly-planted shrubs and plain gravel paths, with a white statue of Jesus in the center. On one side there is a simple covered walkway with bare tree trunks for seats. The remaining three sides are

Visitors to monasteries find that they, too, are expected to keep their appointments to the minute. The cloister garth becomes a useful timepiece: the shadows cast by the walkway columns work like the hands of an enormous sundial, telling the time with considerable accuracy for those who frequently circumnavigate this central chimney of light during the course of the day.

Timekeeping enables punctuality, which enhances the rhythm of the monk's routine and contributes to the stability of the community as a whole.

Stability is one of the principal differences between monastic and secular life: where people living in the world move frequently to pursue careers, attend school, visit family, or simply find a better climate, monasteries stay in the same place, and the members of their community stay there with them. The high degree of permanence and stability offers the cloistered religious a special kind of security and the surroundings that encourage living a spiritual life.

Another special use of the cloister is the processional. Dating back possibly

OPPOSITE:
A second cloister garth at Saint-Pierre Abbey, Solesmes, France, has a classic configuration with a central water feature and four pathways dividing the garden, surrounded by cypresses.

RIGHT:
The hills of Santa Barbara, California, form a backdrop to the perennial cloister garden at Mount Calvary Monastery.

to the Middle Ages, this is an exceptionally beautiful practice that few outsiders
are privileged to see. On ceremonial days
the nuns or monks (and occasionally
both together) line up two by two and
walk, usually singing, through the cloister to the chapel. It is a poignant sight:
habits swaying, they move slowly around
the garth, their voices more and more
muffled as they enter the chapel, until
the cloister returns once more to silence.

A feature common to monasteries is
the statue of the Virgin Mary found in
the southeast corner of the cloister walk.
Depending on the architecture of the
cloister, the style of the statue can vary
from modern abstraction to classical

marble, but the Virgin is always shown
holding the infant Jesus in her arms, and
there are always cut flowers or potted
plants around the base of her statue.
Processions on days dedicated to her,
like the Feast of the Assumption,
invariably end in front of her statue.

Needless to say, there are many variations on the elements of the garth.
Some monasteries have introduced colorful plantings, especially roses and
hydrangeas. Others have more than one
cloister. The Saint-Pierre Abbey in
Solesmes, France, has two—one is a
boxwood parterre designed to be
viewed from above. It is in the shape of
a fleur-de-lis, a reminder that the

glassed in and closed to the interior. The garden is wonderfully serene, the only disturbance coming from the birds that fly back and forth from their nests in the chapel spire that rises high above the garden.

Three-sided cloisters sometimes result from the failure to finish planned buildings, as at Downside Abbey in England, the Abbey of Fleury at Saint-Benoit-sur-Loire, and the second cloister at Solesmes. But whether a cloister garth is completed or not, it remains a wonderful place for contemplation. In the country, where birds swoop in and out looking for worms or places to perch and sing, or in large cities like Rome, where the garth offers a haven from the hubbub without, cloister garths create green oases of safety, simplicity, and purity. The members of the monastic community can touch on that oasis as they pass from one activity to the next, or sit and listen to the stillness as the sunlight marks the time.

OPPOSITE:
A quiet corner of sixteenth-century Burford Priory, Oxon, England.

2

THE SACRISTAN'S CUTTING GARDEN

HE SACRISTAN'S GARDEN, WHICH PROVIDES FLOWERS FOR THE ALTAR OF THE CHAPEL, IS USUALLY ON THE SCRUFFY SIDE. SOME MONASTERIES DO WITHOUT ONE, LIKE THE TYMAWR CONVENT IN WALES, WHERE THE SACRISTAN COLLECTS FROM PATCHES OF WILDFLOWERS OR THE BORDERS OF THE GUEST HOUSE GARDEN. STILL OTHERS SUBSTITUTE POTTED PLANTS FOR THE ALTAR, OUT OF RELUCTANCE TO CUT FLOWERS. MORE OFTEN, HOWEVER, THE CUTTING GARDEN IS TUCKED AWAY IN AN OUT-OF-THE-WAY PLACE.

PRECEDING PAGES:
A monk cuts flowers from the sacristan's cutting garden at Notre Dame Abbey, Le Bec Hellouin, France.

OPPOSITE:
Dahlias are the simple offering in the chapel at Sainte-Cécile Abbey, Solesmes, France.

TO A

FROM

TOP:
A cross i
of St.-Ge
France.

RIGHT:
A single
Monaste
of the Re

ABOVE:
Daffodil
adorn the
Monaste
of the Re
New Yor

TO A **SPIRITUAL BEING,** HAS BEEN COMMON

FROM ANCIENT EGYPT AND GREECE TO THE **PRESENT.**

wildflowers. But in that haven of tranquility it was the perfect offering. More than a flower, it was a symbol that gave rest to the eye and mind.

The nuns at St.-George des Gardes are skilled at placing flowers everywhere. In addition to the chapel, there are simple arrangements of two or three blooms in the visitors' entryway, the refectory, and the guest rooms. They create a sense of tranquility as pervasive as excellent perfume. The concept of offering flowers, as a gift to a spiritual being, has been common to many societies and religions, from ancient Egypt and Greece to the present. In the Catholic countries of the West people often place flowers on shrines to their favorite saints; when fresh flowers aren't available, plastic

ones have the same symbolism. Similarly, on the other side of the world, the small shrines placed at crossroads and gateways in Bali are daily adorned with fresh flowers and simple offerings of food.

Traditionally, flowers have provided symbolic religious references that ordinary people could easily recognize and understand. In Christianity, the Bible describes three aspects of the Christian faith through the symbolic characteristics of flowers; first, the renewal of life or the redemption of our sins; second, the purity and beauty of creation; and third, the fragility and impermanence of our lives on earth. The first derivation for the three aspects can be found in the flowers of springtime, signifying the rebirth and

THE CONCEPT OF OFFERING **FLOWERS**, AS A GIFT TO MANY **SOCİETİES** AND **RELİGİOΠS**,

The act of cutting a flower and placing it in a church gives the flower a whole new meaning. A visitor to the Cistercian convent at St.-George des Gardes, France, appreciated this after a visit to a small refuge. Set in the midst of the woods, so modest as to be practically invisible, stood a small retreat house of elementary design: a simple door, a single window, white-washed walls and a partially translucent corrugated roof that let in a steady light. The furnishings were purely functional. There was a crucifix on the wall, a kneeling prayer stand that took up half the room, and a small wooden table and matching stool in front of the window. There were no rugs on the beige tile floor, but, on a shelf beneath the crucifix, someone had placed the single bloom of a Jerusalem artichoke.

The flower showed that, despite its isolation and simplicity, this building was tended with love. The yellow color of the single bloom carried the whole room and lifted the spirits of those who entered. A closer look revealed the individual character of the particular flower—something that artists such as Georgia O'Keeffe, Robert Mapplethorpe, Bruce Rae, and Christine Simoneau have recognized. As the eye abstracted the shapes of the petals and stamens, individual details of that bloom stood out like identifying marks among the characteristics of the species. The petals were slightly deformed, and the coloration was faulty: no florist would put that Jerusalem artichoke in the display window. In the hedgerow, too, it would go unnoticed, just an ordinary bloom among a multitude of

TOP:
A candle arrangement at the Monastery of Our Lady of the Resurrection, New York.

LEFT:
One simple arrangement at a shrine of Mary and the Holy Child at Notre Dame des Gardes Abbey, St.-George des Gardes, France.

ABOVE:
Roses adorn the guest house entry at St.-George des Gardes.

redemption as in Solomon's Song of Songs 2:11-12:

See! The winter is past; the rains are over and gone. Flowers appear on the earth; the season of singing has come, the cooing of doves is heard in our land.

The symbols for purity, beauty, and sweetness can also be found in Solomon's Song of Songs 2:1-2:

I am the rose of Sharon, a lily of the Valleys. Like a lily among thorns is my darling among maidens.

The meaning of the text has two parts. Christ likens himself to flowers directly by, "I am the rose of Sharon, a lily of the valleys," and His church, "my darling," as purity among the impure or a lily among thorns. (Incidentally, the rose of Sharon is not *Hypericum calycinum* or *Hibiscus syriacus* but rather the plentiful narcissus or tulips which grow on the plains of Sharon, and the lily of the valley is thought to be a blue hyacinth that is abundant in that region.)

Ultimately, flowers also symbolize the transitory nature of our lives, as in Isaiah 40:6-8:

All men are like grass, and all their glory is like the flowers of the field. The grass withers and the flowers fall, because the breath of the Lord blows on them. Surely the people are grass. The grass withers and the flowers fall, but the word of our God stands forever.

Symbolic meanings can guide the sacristan in his choice of which flowers to cut for the altar, but at any given time the determining factor is whatever happens to be in bloom. When the season provides a wide selection, preference is given to those flowers whose colors harmonize with the priests' vestments.

OPPOSITE:
A Jerusalem artichoke blossom brightens a tiny prayer room in the woods at Notre Dame des Gardes Abbey, St.-George des Gardes, France.

LEFT:
The cutting garden at the Monastery of Our Lady of the Resurrection, New York.

At Whitsuntide, red peonies are chosen to represent the tongues of fire that descended on the apostles at Pentecost; red also symbolizes the blood of Christ and the blood of the martyrs on their feast days. During the solemn seasons of Advent and Lent, flowers are not placed in the chapel except on the third Sunday of Advent and the fourth Sunday of Lent, when violet blooms are used to signify penitence and watchfulness. Green, the color of nature and therefore symbolic of God's bountiful-ness, appears at Trinity, while black is only used on Good Friday and for funeral services. The most important color of all—white—symbolizes joy and Jesus' spotless purity: it is the color of Christmas, Epiphany and Easter. White is also the color associated with angels and the robes of those saints who were not martyred, of weddings and confirmations, and of the Blessed Virgin Mary.

Throughout the Middle Ages, when flower symbolism was especially preva-

The round stone chapter house at the Abbey of Regina Laudis, Connecticut, stands behind a flower cutting garden.

lent, many plants were connected with some aspect of Mary's life or person. The large number of these connections, and their not infrequent obscurity, testifies to the Virgin's popularity, which survives in the large number of plants known as "Our Lady's," "Lady's," or "Maiden." Sometimes a single such name refers to various plants. "Our Lady's Cushion," for example, can refer to *Arabis albida*, *Armeria vulgaris*, *Chrysoplenium oppositifolium*, *Lotus corniculatus, Saxifraga hypnoides* or *Saxifraga umbrosa*. Similarly "Lady's Cushion" signifies *Anthyllis Vulneraria, Armeria maritima, Centauria nigra,* and *Knautia arvensis.* The symbolism is very old—early portrayals of St. Fiacre, for instance, depict him in his forest garden by a chapel to the Virgin decorated with cut flowers.

An account of the cutting garden would be incomplete without mentioning the symbolism of the common blue passiflora or passion flower. In 1610, an Augustinian friar from

Mexico named Emanuel de Villegas ascribed to each part of the flower a symbolic value related to the suffering and death of Jesus. The pointed leaves represent the spears that pierced his side as he hung on the Cross; they are grouped in fives, for his five sacred wounds. The plant's unusual tendrils remind us of the cords that bound Jesus' hands, while the pillar protruding from the flower symbolizes the Cross. The ten petals of the bloom stand for the ten apostles who remained faithful to their Master (the exceptions are Peter, who denied knowing him three times in the course of the night, and Judas, who betrayed him for thirty pieces of silver). The passion flower's crimson styles symbolize the bloodied nails, while the exaggerated stamens recall the hammers that drove the nails into Jesus' hands and feet. The circle surrounding the pillar is said to represent the crown of thorns; the radiating filaments point to the glory of God. Finally, the flower's distinctive fragrance represents the perfumed oil with which Jesus was anointed at Bethany the week before his crucifixion.

OPPOSITE:
Geraniums, peonies, roses, irises, and pansies flourish in the garden at Burnham Abbey, Berkshire, England.

ABOVE:
A border in full bloom at Burford Priory, Oxon, England.

3

THE PHYSIC OR HERB GARDEN

ERBAL REMEDIES THAT WERE ONCE A VITAL PART OF MONASTIC LIFE ARE NO LONGER NEEDED NOW BY EITHER MONKS OR THE LOCAL COMMUNITIES THEY SERVE. IT IS RARE TO FIND A MEDICINAL HERB OR PHYSIC GARDEN IN TODAY'S MONASTERIES. THE WONDERFUL SERIES OF BOOKS, WRITTEN BY ELLIS PETERS ON BROTHER CADFAEL, WHOSE KNOWLEDGE OF HERBS SAVED LIVES AND SOLVED MURDER MYSTERIES, IS FICTION OF THE PAST. FOR MONASTERIES, KEEPING ABREAST OF MODERN SCIENCE HAS MEANT REPLACING LABOR INTENSIVE HERBAL REMEDIES WITH THE QUICK CURES OF PHARMACOLOGY.

PRECEDING PAGES:
The enclosed garden at Burnham Abbey, Berkshire, England, features several herbs and roses, and an espaliered fig tree.

OPPOSITE:
Dill, wormwood, borage, and elecampane form part of an herb garden in front of espaliered pear trees at Convent of the Incarnation, Fairacres, Oxfordshire, England.

CHRISTIAN ERA AND IN THE MIDDLE AGES, MONASTERIES

WHICH MEANT THAT THE **HERB GARDEN**

WHOLE **COMMUNITY'S** WELL-BEING.

ers of herbs; they revered plants as part of their folklore, their holy sites were often adjacent to old oak trees or unusually shaped rocks, and their shamans used herbs along with astrology and parts of animals to conjure spells and guarantee good luck. But the barbarians gave little thought to documenting the qualities of herbs or to preserving plant specimens.

Like arks in the stormy sea of those centuries, monasteries carried the records of learning to safe haven. They assumed the task of collecting, preserving and copying manuscripts of all kinds, including medical texts. Monastic libraries were not just centers of Biblical and theological research but safe repositories for the literature, philosophy, and science of ancient Egypt, Mesopotamia, Palestine, China, India, and Arabia, in addition to Greece and Rome. We know from a 3,500-year old papyrus discovered by George Ebers in 1874, for example, that some 800 drugs were known to the ancient Egyptians, among them garlic, onion, fenugreek, mustard, thyme, anise, cassia, fennel, cardamom, saffron, poppy seed, and coriander. In ancient India, cannabis and henbane were used as anesthetics, while the Chinese grew rhubarb, aconite, and opium for the same purpose.

Much of this information had been

IN THE **EARLY CENTURIES** OF THE

FUNCTIONED AS LOCAL **HEALTH** ORGANIZATIONS

WAS AN **ESSENTIAL** PART OF THE

The physic garden may be gone from today's monasteries, but the underlying spiritual reason for its existence lives on in other forms. For Christians, to love one's neighbor as oneself is the second of the two greatest commandments (Matthew 22: 39). The Rule of St. Benedict, in the chapter titled "The Tools of Good Work," reinforces this teaching under the rubric of caring for the aged and infirm both inside the monastery and in the world outside. In a later passage, St. Benedict clarifies: "The care of the sick is to be given priority over everything else, so that they are indeed served as Christ would be served."

In the early centuries of the Christian era and in the Middle Ages, monasteries functioned as local health organizations, which meant that the herb garden was an essential part of the whole community's well-being. This was due in large part to the role historically played by monasteries in preserving and advancing medical knowledge, beginning in roughly 476 A.D., when barbarian tribes invaded the collapsing Roman Empire from the north and east, and extending through the four centuries of cultural stagnation and physical decay that used to be known as the Dark Ages. The barbarians themselves were not indifferent to the healing pow-

TOP:
Peonies at Stanbrook Abbey, Worcester, England.

LEFT:
Early primroses at Burford Priory, Oxon, England.

ABOVE:
The formal French garden at Saint-Pierre Abbey, Solesmes, France.

collected by the Greeks and housed in the great library of Alexandria, Egypt, a unique source of knowledge from its foundation in the third century B.C. until 640 A.D., when after surviving depredation by the Romans in 272 and 391 A.D., it was completely destroyed by the Muslims. In it one could find the Hippocratic Collection written in the fifth century B.C. on the Greek island of Kos; the books in which Galen explained his famous and immensely influential theory of the four humors; Pliny the Elder's encyclopedic *Historia naturalis* from 77 A.D.; and the works of Dioscorides, the first scientist of medicinal herbs, whose vast second-century treatise *De materia medica* described medicines derived from six hundred plants, thirty-five animals, and ninety minerals, and became the basic

text for pharmacology for the next fifteen hundred years. Without the monasteries, neither Dioscorides' nor many of the other key manuscripts of antiquity would have survived those dark centuries.

In order to fulfill this role, monasteries had to develop ways to reproduce texts. In ancient Greece and Rome, and in Christian Europe prior to the invention of movable type, this meant copying manuscripts, word for word, by hand. From the earliest times specially trained monks were used for this purpose. We know that these scribes were present in monasteries founded by St. Pachomius, who died in 346, and by the fourth-century Desert Fathers. In the same period St. Jerome made use of them in preparing his Latin translation of the Bible. When it became clear that income could be

derived from the sale of copied texts, the scribes were considered a valuable part of the monastic economy. The room where they worked—the scriptorium—was divided into areas according to individual expertise, for the making of books was not a simple matter. Scribes copied the text itself while rubrics were supplied by a rubricator, and ornate initials were added by the miniators. In the bigger monasteries, the scriptoria could grow quite large.

Work in the scriptorium was exact-ing. It required a rare combination of knowledge and patience, especially when translation and interpretation were involved in addition to simple copying. To promote these qualities, St. Benedict encouraged the monks of his own monastery at Monte Cassino to study the sciences, especially medicine. Not everyone followed St. Benedict's example. In order to fight pagan super-stitions regarding plants, Burchard, Bishop of Worms decreed in 1020 A.D. that when harvesting herbs, people

should focus their thoughts on religion instead of the study of the stars, not to mention pagan folklore. "In the gathering of medicinal herbs," he wrote, "save only the creed and the paternoster." Even more suspicious of medicinal herbs was St. Bernard. He joined a group of Benedictines that had broken off from the mother monastery at Molesme in 1098 A.D. in order to found a stricter order, which became known as the Cistercians (from the Latin name for Citeaux, the swampy area where they settled). As the spiritual leader of the new order, St. Bernard prohibited his fellow Cistercians from studying any kind of medicine, prescribing prayer and love alone for the treatment of the sick. But again, Burchard and St. Bernard were exceptions. Some years after St. Benedict's death one of Monte Cassino's monks, Constantine of Africa, became an important Latin translator of Greek medical texts that had survived in Arabic. Still later, around 1140 A.D.,

Archbishop Raimundo of Toledo created an institute to translate Arabic medical texts into Latin. It is important to remember, nonetheless, that whatever the scribe's level of erudition, the principal guides for work in the scriptorium, as everywhere in the monastery, were the virtues of obedience, humility, and perseverance as set down in the Rule, for St. Benedict had written: "Whoever exalts himself will be humbled, and he who humbles himself will be exalted."

We know quite a bit about the connection between spiritual life and herbal medicine from stories and accounts that have been handed down by monastic writers. One of the oldest is told by the Venerable Bede, who died in 735. Bede, a monk at the Northumbrian Abbeys of St. Peter at Wearmouth and St. Paul at Jarrow,

invented the Anno Domini system of dating, wrote about the history of Christianity in England, and made such important contributions to theology that he was proclaimed a Doctor of the Church. In telling a story about St. Cuthbert of Lindisfarne, Bede reveals the extent to which the medical treatment of his day was influenced by spiritual, even mystical, experiences. The story goes that, as a child, St. Cuthbert suffered from such a painful tumor on his knee that he had to be carried by servants. One day he had a vision of an angel in white, riding on a horse. The angel examined the tumor and told the boy: "Boil some wheaten flour in milk and bathe the tumor with it hot, and you will be healed." Naturally, the cure worked; within a few days, the tumor had disappeared.

Not long after, on Christmas Day in the year 800, Pope Leo III crowned Charlemagne Emperor of the Holy

OPPOSITE:
Rosemary, lavender, dill, and borage surround a sundial in the herb garden at the Monastery of Our Lady of the Rock, Washington.

LEFT:
The enclosed herb garden at the Monastery of Our Lady of the Rock, Washington.

Roman Empire. Charlemagne was a Frankish warrior who had spent years fighting for control of the Empire and protecting the Papacy from the Lombards. He was also sufficiently intrigued by gardening to have included a number of like-minded monks in his court, in particular Alcuin of York, an enthusiastic student and collector of botanical specimens (Charlemagne may also have exchanged plants with a monk named Benedict, from Aniane). He translated his interest into imperial policy in an edict of 812 A.D. called the *Capitulare de villis*, which specifies some seventy-three plants, nuts and fruit trees—many of them medicinal—that

could be grown in the 250 "counts" of his kingdom.

We have an idea of the kinds of herbs that were common in monastic physic gardens of this period from the pen of Walafrid Strabo ("Squinter"), monk and theologian of Reichenau, Germany. Around 840 A.D. Strabo wrote a beautiful poem called "Hortulus" in which he lovingly describes clearing a garden of stinging nettles and preparing the soil to plant sage, southernwood, wormwood, fennel, poppy, clary, mint, pennyroyal, celery, betony, agrimony, tansy, catmint, and radish. Strabo introduces his herbs the way a mother might speak of her

children, praising their qualities without neglecting the occasional blemish. It is worth noting that in the Middle Ages, the Latin word *herba* (herb) designated most plants except trees.

Three more descriptions of monastic gardens from the tenth to the thirteenth centuries suggest the variety of herbs in common use. The first is from *The Leech Book* ("leech" in the old English sense of "physician"). Composed between 926 and 946 A.D. by an English monk named Bald and written down by the scribe Cild, it contains recipes for herbal remedies using mugwort, plantain, wood betony, yarrow, vervaine, violets, and Saint-

John's-wort. The second, the *Lacunga*, an herbal "charm" book from the eleventh century, gives medicinal uses for plaintain, chamomile, nettle, chervil, lamb's cress, cockspur grass, and crab apples. Finally, in the *De naturis rerum* written by Abbot Alexander of Necham, England at the turn of the thirteenth century, we find a description of an ideal garden containing parsley, cost, fennel, southernwood, coriander, sage, savoy, hyssop, mint, rue, dittany, smallage, pellitory, lettuce, garden cress, peonies, and soup herbs like beets, herb mercury, orach, sorrel, and mallows. The Abbot also prescribes borage, pennyroyal, saffron,

and thyme for medicinal use.

Finally, we can turn to the scientific names of plants for clues to which of them were commonly grown in monasteries. The key is the Latin word *officinalis* ("workshop"), which in the Middle Ages also meant "of or pertaining to a monastery." (It lives on in the English word "officinal," meaning "kept in stock by a druggist...or recognized by the pharmacopeia.") Thus we find that the Latin term for marshmallow is *Althea officinalis*; borage, *Borago*

o.; marigold, *Calendula o.*; fumitory, *Fumaria o.*; hyssop, *Hyssopus o.*; jasmine, *Jasminum o.*; lavender, *Lavendula o.*; lemon balm, *Melissa o.*; peony, *Paeonia o.*; lungwort, *Pulmonaria o.*; apothecary rose, *Rosa gallica var. o.*; rosemary, *Rosmarinus o.*; sage, *Salvia o.*; snapwort, *Saponaria o.*; comfrey, *Symphytum o.*; valerian, *Valeriana o*; and vervain, *Verbena o.* A variant of *officinalis* is *officinale*, as in lovage or *Levisticum officinale*, and dandelion or *Taraxacum officinale*. The names indi-

cate that all of these herbs were culti-vated in monastic gardens.

Today, there is a resurgence to look at plants for their healing qualities, as society turns to a more holistic view of treating health problems. The herbalist recognizes the "active ingredient" in a plant is usually combined with several other ingredients which help to bal-ance the side effects. In pharmacology, the "active ingredient" is so isolated that other drugs have to be prescribed to treat the side effects. The medieval herbalist used dandelions, for example, as a diuretic. We now know that dan-delion leaves have a high potassium content, which gives them an advan-tage over modern synthetic diuretics that tend to reduce bodily potassium drastically, thereby creating an addi-tional deficiency that must be treated in its own right. Often despised as an annoying intruder in our lawns, the dandelion has other unsung benefits as

well. The leaves contain lutein, violax-anthin, bitters, vitamins A, B, C, and D, and iron, while the root has insulin, sterols, triterpenoids, bitters, pectin, glycosides, and asparagine—agents that treat poisoning and rheumatism and have laxative properties. "Poor man's coffee" is made from roasted dandelion roots, and the flowers are the major ingredient of dandelion wine.

The proper know-how was required to extract the healing qualities from this and other plants grown in monasteries, where one monk was usually assigned to study the preparation and use of each herb. Because some herbs are potentially poisonous, the monk had to have a very thorough knowledge of how to harvest, store, and administer them. Properly handled, they could be eaten fresh in salads, dried and mixed with a base to form a rudimentary pill, drunk in teas and tinctures, and applied to the skin by massage or in compresses of salves and ointments. Liquids were prepared by infusion, that is, by pouring boiling water on the chopped plant; by decoction, in which they were boiled in a non-metallic pot over low heat; or by maceration, whereby the herbs were left to steep for a while in cold water or alcohol, which was eventually warmed and strained. Beeswax or lard provided the base for

ointments into which the herbs were mixed directly or in the form of tinctures and oils. Since the ideal base was whatever substance best dissolved the prescribed essence, it varied from the milk of cows, sheep, and goats, to cider, verjuice (sour crab apple cider), ale, and wine, to the oils of walnut, almond, rosemary, and lavender.

As for how herbs were grown in the physic garden, we find a partial answer in the plan for a monastery drawn up for Abbot Gozbert of St. Gall, in Switzerland, around 820 A.D., six years after the death of Charlemagne. Although the monastery was never built, the plan is a beautiful illustration of the intimate relationship between monastic life and gardening. The dimensions of the buildings and their connection to the gardens are carefully specified. Clustered around the physician's quarters are the physic garden (to the north), the infirmary (to the east), and the bloodletting room (to the south). The gardeners' quarters are just south of

the flower beds, the cemetery is to the west, the goose- and chicken-yard is to the east, and the latrine is to the south—the latter two being handily located sources of manure and night soil.

Although the St. Gall plan called for some herbs to be grown in the vegetable garden, the majority would have been planted in the physic garden in separate raised beds, one species to each bed. The garden would have been enclosed by walls, the buildings of the monastery proper, or perhaps a wooden stockade.

The St. Gall plan specifies plantings of fennel, white lily, sage, rue, pennyroyal, fenugreek, peppermint, rosemary, corn-flag, cumin, lovage, roses, watercress, savory, tansy, and—surprisingly—kidney beans. There were to have been sixteen beds in two lines of eight beds each, a practical design that aided iden-tification. The physician could instruct a novice to fetch some rue, for exam-ple, specifying that it was the plant with the yellow flowers in the fourth bed nearest the infirmary, and have

some expectation that the correct plant would be delivered.

Today, monasteries that continue growing herbs usually incorporate them into the vegetable garden. A noticeable exception is the convent of Our Lady of the Rock on Shaw Island, off Seattle, Washington. Behind the nuns' lovely enclosed herb garden is a wood of magnificent lichen-covered fir trees; in front is a pasture with grazing cows and llamas. The herbs are put to a variety of uses. Fresh or dried, they liven the community's salads, soups, and casseroles, and a hot mustard is prepared from nasturtium capers. The nuns use dried calendula petals as a saffron substitute and to decorate cakes, and they grow four different kinds of lavender for sachets to freshen cupboards and drawers. The nuns also make a spray of basil, vinegar, and water to keep flies off their cattle in the summer, and they use mugwort to make a moth-deterrent for their clothes. When they are in bloom, the sacristan collects herb flowers for the church.

Sister Felicitas has primary responsibility for the garden on the day of this particular visit. She makes a "sweet herb" tea out of whatever happens to be doing well at the moment, well aware of its medicinal benefits. She observes:

> When you make a tea and it has rosemary, sage, camomile, and peppermint, you know that some of those herbs are antibiotic and some antibacterial. You are confident that you are not invading the body; it is a minimal intervention that helps keep the body in balance. This way of using plants is perfectly safe. We don't really get into medicinal herbs because it is quite

specialized, and it would be irre-
sponsible to work with them without being very knowledgeable.

She goes on to explain that at least
three of the thirty-seven herbs they
grow—black hellebore, monk's hood,
and foxglove—are quite poisonous
but that medieval monks would have
known how to use them.

For Sister Felicitas and guests at the
monastery, the simple experience of working in the garden or simply spending time
there has a healing power. She says:

I find that even in stressful times
you cannot worry while working in
a garden, even though the garden
seems so overwhelming that you
will never catch up with it, and
never get everything done. Still, I
feel incredible peace working there.

I think gardens are an inex-
haustible source of analogies about
life and the relationships of things.
These analogies come to me constantly when I'm gardening. It is a
mode of thinking that is very

LEFT:
*A solitary prayer seat
in Downside Abbey,
Stratton-on-the-Fosse,
Somerset, England.*

*important in my spirituality to get
away from the purely rational.*

*There is in a garden an order
that the gardener creates in coop-
eration with nature. There is an
energy that emanates from the
plants. As soon as I step into the
garden I feel it. It's like going into
a chapel where people have prayed
a lot: you feel a certain energy
from that prayer. The same thing
happens in the garden except that
the energy comes from nature, but*

it comes from an ordered nature.

*The innate, inherent contra-
diction of any garden is that if you
don't tend it, nature takes over and
it reverts back to nature. Here is
an analogy that came to me the
other day: we are just like gardens,
in that if we don't take care of our
spiritual life and identity—if we
don't try to rise above our
instincts—then we revert to that
level, from which it is hard to rise.*

4

THE

VEGETABLE

GARDEN

O WATCH THE SUN RISE OVER THE BEAUTIFULLY TENDED VEGETABLE GARDEN AT SAINT MARY'S ABBEY IN WEST MALLING, ENGLAND, IS TO HAVE A NEW APPRECIATION FOR THE IMPORTANCE OF A UTILITARIAN PLACE. NESTLED COMFORTABLY WITHIN THE MONASTERY WALLS, THIS GARDEN HAS A KIND OF DIGNITY OF ITS OWN THAT REFLECTS THE SPIR-ITUAL CONNECTION OF GARDENING WITH MONASTIC LIFE. AS ONE OF THE NUNS EXPLAINS: "I THINK THEORETICALLY THE VEGETABLE GARDEN IS VERY IMPORTANT, BECAUSE OF THE IMPORTANCE THAT

PRECEDING PAGES:
Morning at the vegetable garden of Saint Mary's Abbey, West Malling, Kent, England.

OPPOSITE:
The orderly vegetable garden at the Convent of the Incarnation, Fairacres, Oxfordshire, England.

WORKING WITH **PLANTS,** ONE GETS TO KNOW THEI

A COMMODITY. THE GARDENER BECOMES **ROOTED** TO

Benedictines give to manual labor. Working on the land has special significance for us because the idea of humility is fundamental to our Rule, and "humility" comes from humus, or soil; the two are deeply connected.

We are trying to be stewards of our environment. It is part of the Benedictine life to nurture the environment and to be stewards of all the utensils of the monastery, and that includes the land. We are stable. We have a vow of stability so we stay with our little piece of land for the rest of our lives.

We lead a spiritual life that is balanced between work, prayer, and study. I believe it is important to have a balance in our lives between the body, the soul, and the mind.

Working with plants, one gets to know their essence and understand that they are not just a commodity. The gardener becomes rooted to the ground, which is part of God's creation. Everything around us is God's creation ... [This is why] we have to revere everything in the earth.

At first glance, the connection between "humility" and "soil" might seem forced, but their Latin roots reveal the connection, humus means "soil,

TOP:
Lettuce.

LEFT:
A nun tends the vegetable garden at The Abbey of Regina Laudis, Connecticut.

ABOVE:
A monk takes care of the sheep at the Monastery of Our Lady of the Resurrection, New York.

SSENCE AND UNDERSTAND THAT THEY ARE NOT JUST

HE GROUND, WHICH IS PART OF **GOD'S CREATION.**

TOP:
Zucchini.

RIGHT:
Cabbage.

ground, or earth," and *humilitas* means "nearness to the ground." Monastic life underscores the notion that by humbling himself, the monk becomes fertile again, in the same way that the soil he handles with respect and reverence encourages the growth of good, healthy plants. The monk holds a respect for soil as an essential element of God's creation.

We have already seen that according to St. Benedict the way to achieve "heavenly exaltation" on earth is through the practice of humility. In the Rule, St. Benedict uses the image of the ladder to represent our life, and the motion of climbing up or down repre-

sents our actions. St. Benedict's twelve steps to humility are the rungs on this ladder. When we act pridefully, we are climbing down, but humility carries us up. The monk who humbly ascends will attain "that love of God which, being perfect, drives out all fear." In the monastery, humility is therefore not a state of failure but a journey that brings us closer to God.

Visitors are often struck by the monastic community's profound awareness of the birds and animals that share their living space. These creatures are treated with the same respect

as the soil, as essential elements in God's creation and a gift that has been entrusted to the care of the community.

This attitude has ecological lessons from which all of us can learn. Because monasteries "stay where they are" and their members take a vow of stability, they do not recklessly exploit their land, assuming that they can move on and leave the mess for another generation to clean up. Because they are in situ for the long term, they take care not to upset the balance of nature and they plan ahead for their environment's future. Consequently, most monasteries practice organic gardening. They rely on microorganisms to release nutrients from organic matter into the soil, thus keeping it healthy. They believe that the chemical alternative is successful only in the short term, but that in the long term it will lead to the destruction of the living earth, because the ever higher concentrations of chemicals needed to sustain production levels will kill off the earth's microorganisms in a downward spiral that ends with toxic soil and toxic food.

The community at West Malling turned away from chemical gardening twenty years ago: today, their vegetable beds are full of organic material, a fact not lost on visitors. As the nuns will readily admit, showing visitors around the vegetable garden is their quiet way of promoting the virtues of organic gardening. This includes green manure techniques—that is, raising crops of red clover (*Trifolium pratense*), fava beans (*Vicia faba*), alfalfa (*Medicago sativa*), and winter vetch (*Vicia villosa*)—plants that fix the nitrogen in the soil. Before they grow "woody" they are dug back into the

OPPOSITE:
Beautifully ripened tomatoes from Notre Dame des Gardes Abbey, St.-George des Gardes, France.

topsoil, where in decomposition they release their nitrogen which had previously leached too deep for ordinary roots to reach. Sometimes the nuns leave these plants to flower so they can attract bees and insects before being cut up for compost. There is something attractive about this variety of uses. As one nun comments:

I like the kitchen garden because you have to be so flexible. If it rains tomorrow there will be weeds all over the place, and we will have to hoe those in. You have to deal with each day as it comes: that means living in the present moment and not trying to control things too much.

At Mepkin Abbey near Charleston, South Carolina the monks have developed a garden compost tea they call "Earth Healer," a combination of chicken manure and white pine shavings from a local furniture factory. It can be added directly to the soil or used as a tea base for liquid manure, which is

especially good for houseplants. The robust health of their plants is good validation for their product, which they supply to gardeners outside the monastery as well.

There are many such examples from around the world. At the monastery of Saint-Benoit-sur-Loire, the monks use liquid compost made by decomposing nettles in drums full of water—a system invented by one of the brothers. Seaweed is good for soil structure, is high in potassium, and contains alginic acid, which attracts bacteria essential to the decomposition cycle. The nuns of Our Lady of the Rock near Seattle use seaweed from the nearby shore and mix it directly with the soil or cut it up and add it to the compost. Their compost heaps also receive manure from the convent's hens and cows. Such conventional composting methods embrace a variety of substances, which allows monasteries to recycle kitchen refuse, weeds, cut grass, and even socks.

Control of garden pests is always a

challenge. Aphids, wood lice, snails, slugs, white flies, and millipedes must be addressed with some ingenuity if they are to be held in check by natural predators. At Burford Abbey in Oxon, England, the monks, with the help of visitors, build mounds of twigs from old trees they have taken down. As one of the monks explains, the stacks of twigs are insect habitats:

> They attract thousands of lady-bugs to hibernate, and on a warm spring day the ladybugs come out and sit on top of the stacks. It looks as if they had been painted red, there are so many of them.

Ladybugs and hover flies, which prey successfully on aphids, can also be attracted by flat flowering plants like French marigolds (*Tagetes*). In its beautiful vegetable garden, the Abbey of Regina Laudis, in Bethlehem, Connecticut, plants marigold as a companion to its six or seven yearly crops of lettuce. Another handy method for controlling slugs is frogs and hens. The sisters at West Malling provide their garden with frog access points by building low walls around the pond. Slugs and snails are most active in the morning and early evening; an evening visitor to Our Lady of the Rock once helped collect over five dozen slugs, which were fed immediately to the monastery's delighted hens.

The organic garden process recycles the unwanted back into the useful and necessary, a familiar message in the monastery. The beauty of the vegetable garden lies in its very ordinariness: the well trodden path with the bumps and puddles that the foot so quickly adjusts to, the functional design of forks, spades, and hoes, the smell of the turned soil—these have been the same for centuries. Intimate

familiarity with the ordinary, even in the less organic form of diesel exhaust from a tractor, enables one to experience it anew, as something special. One of the monks of En Calcat, in Dourgne, France, explains what this simple place means to him:

This is the most beautiful building here, where the tractor lives and the pitchforks. Oh, how I *love it! All of this, this is a monk's place, and it's really my favorite. Here we have the compost, and the shed where we repair the machinery and the bikes. We have a carpentry shop and a garage around the corner. All of these spaces are very practical. The vegetable garden has been in use for a hundred*

Tomatoes and gourds surround a small chapel at Notre Dame des Gardes Abbey, St.-George des Gardes, France.

years—that's where the compost comes in. And there is no symbolic meaning to it at all. It's just a living space. That's what delights me.

Functional buildings like this may lack symbolism, but they are often adorned with a small statue of Our Lady above the entrance or a crucifix above the rows of hand tools. At Notre Dame des Gardes Abbey in St.-George des Gardes, France, there is a tiny chapel in the vegetable garden, big enough for only one or two people to kneel in prayer. It stands right in the middle of the tomatoes, with its double door open to the garden.

In the beginning, of course, monastic vegetable gardens served the idea

that each community should be self-sustaining. The example originally set by the Desert Fathers was encouraged by St. Benedict, who wrote: "For then truly are they monks, if they live by the work of their hands, as did our Fathers and the Apostles." As we have already seen, St. Benedict stressed the importance of a balance within a spiritual life of manual labor and prayer.

Some monasteries nevertheless took exception to the schedule of up to seven hours of labor daily in harmony with the liturgical cycle. By the twelfth century, the monks at Cluny in France had decided that prayer and singing psalms were their proper work and they began employing lay brothers and servants to work the land. This arrangement over the years introduced a distinction between choir monks and lay brothers, in which the former tended towards intellectual pursuits while the latter assumed the burden of manual labor. The issue came before the Second Vatican Council in the early 1960s, and

LEFT:
*An entrance to
the vegetable garden
at the Monastery of
Our Lady of the
Resurrection,
New York.*

the Church decided to let the lay brothers system come to an end by attrition.

Although the Council's intention was to eradicate unnecessary distinctions between the monks, some people saw in this decision the beginning of a decline in the importance of working the land. The most decisive reason for the declining pursuit of self-sufficiency in monasteries, however, is the growth of modern agribusiness. Today's farms have to be much larger than the farms of the past if they are to be profitable, and recently monasteries have generally found that it makes more economic sense to lease their land to local farmers than to work it themselves. At the same time, government regulations on the raising of livestock have become more stringent, making it inconvenient for many monasteries to continue keeping sheep and cows. Monasteries usually retain ownership of their land, to act as a buffer zone around them as well as maintaining an income, but fewer monks are themselves engaged

in farming or animal husbandry.

In the 1980s this change began to extend to labor intensive vegetable gardens, too, as many monasteries decided to cut back their own vegetable growing and buy local produce instead. Many monasteries grassed over or created car parks out of their former vegetable gardens but two examples stand out for what was left behind when the traditional practices were abandoned. At Downside Abbey in England, exceptionally long yew hedges are all that is left of the former vegetable garden they once enclosed, while at Sainte Scholastique Abbey in Dourgne, France, the vegetable garden has been grassed over and incorporated into a remarkable romantic landscape designed and built between 1892 and 1911 by the Toulouse landscape architect Paul Bonnamy.

The decision to give up self-suffi-ciency can be difficult. Several of the religious lamented the loss of the farming and vegetable gardening that had been such an integral part of their lives. The nuns of Tymawr Convent in Wales kept going until they simply could not find enough help to maintain their production of butter and cheese; then, to make matters worse, new EEC regulations required them to rebuild their cow sheds, which they could ill afford. "It just quietly came to an end," said one of the nuns, who had worked on the farm since the early 1950s:

I found that working in the fields, working the land, working with the animals with all that space and sky, it all melded in with the life of prayer, which is what I really wanted, without anything jarring. I just found that it became a very harmonious whole and there was as much prayer going on out in the

fields as there was in the chapel.

We grew all our vegetables. We never bought anything. We grew enough potatoes to last the year round, and fruit as well. In the early days, before freezers, you ate a lot of rhubarb when there was rhubarb, and when the raspberries were in you ate a lot of raspberries. When the cows calved we had extra rich milk and lots of cream. I loved living like that, living and eating in rhythm with the seasons.

One of the big things I learned was how to go along with nature. If there was a drought and one crop failed, another one flourished because of the very same drought. In all, over a period of four or five years, the whole thing balanced out. You could not really control it. It was lovely because I felt I could lose control and go along with what the Lord provided by way of weather and help. That was a very big spiritual lesson.

There are spiritual lessons to be learned from working the land and from the beginning monks grew their own food. While living in Bethlehem in the year 390 A.D., St. Jerome wrote an account of St. Hilarion's visit to the site of the late St. Anthony's hermitage in the desert. After three days of traveling through the desert he was received by two men, one of whom— named Isaac—had attended St. Anthony when he was alive. This Isaac is reported to have said:

Here, so they said, Anthony himself used to sing, pray, work, and rest when weary. Those vines and shrubs were planted by his own hand; that garden bed is his own design. This pool for watering the garden was made by him after much toil. That hoe was handled by him for many years.

You see this garden with its shrubs and green vegetables... About three years ago it was ravaged by a troop of wild asses. One

of their leaders was bidden by Anthony to stand still while he thrashed the animals' sides with a stick and wanted to know why they devoured what they had not sown. And ever afterwards, excepting the water which they were accustomed to come and drink, they never touched anything, not a bush or a vegetable.

The symbolism of the vegetables is poignant, because the Desert Fathers offered them to their visitors as a special welcome, denying themselves the pleasure of this relative delicacy and limiting their diet to barley bread, dried beans, and figs. The monks at twelfth-century Cluny fared better. They ate two meals a day. The main meal had three courses: dried beans; cheese or fish on Thursdays, Sundays, and feast days; and whatever vegetable was in season. The vegetables were usually cooked in fat and seasoned with salt and pepper.

To see what vegetables were grown in the middle ages, a detailed list of plants provided by St. Hildegard of Bingen (1098-1179), most likely reflects what was grown in the gardens of her monastery. Many of them were known to the ancient Greeks and Romans: the broad bean (*Vicia faba*), cabbage and coleworts (*Brassica oleracea*), cucumber (*Cucumis sativus*), garlic (*Allium sativum*), leeks (*Allium porrum*), lettuce (*Lactuca sativa*), onions (*Allium cepa*), peas (*Pisumsativum*), radish (*Raphanus sativus*), shallots (*Allium ascalonicum*), and skirret (*Sium sisarum*). (It is worth noting here that some of the varieties we take for granted today, like Cos lettuce, originated on the Greek island of Kos; it is because it was so popular among the Romans that we also call it Romaine lettuce.) St. Hildegard also

OPPOSITE:
A prize gourd from Abbey of Bellefontaine, Begrolles-En-Mauges, France.

5

ORCHARDS

AND

VINEYARDS

least two varieties of vegetable: a kind of pea with a purple bloom known as Blue Pod Capucijners and the endive we call Belgian but known in French as *barbe de capuchin* (Capuchin monk's beard). The greatest name of all in this field is Gregor Mendel, the Augustinian brother who founded the science of genetics. Appointed abbot of the monastery at Brünn (today Brno in Austria) in 1860, Mendel still found time to continue his experiment with crossbreeding specimens from among the 21,000 pea plants in the community's gardens and greenhouses. Working with the common garden pea within the peaceful confines of a monastery garden, the Abbot made discoveries that led to the concept of dominant and recessive hereditary traits. Although his work was passed over by his contemporaries, it was the foundation for the extraordinary developments in biogenetics, posing serious ethical questions as we enter the third millennium.

5

ORCHARDS

AND

VINEYARDS

of their leaders was bidden by Anthony to stand still while he thrashed the animals' sides with a stick and wanted to know why they devoured what they had not sown. And ever afterwards, excepting the water which they were accustomed to come and drink, they never touched anything, not a bush or a vegetable.

The symbolism of the vegetables is poignant, because the Desert Fathers offered them to their visitors as a special welcome, denying themselves the pleasure of this relative delicacy and limiting their diet to barley bread, dried beans, and figs. The monks at twelfth-century Cluny fared better. They ate two meals a day. The main meal had three courses: dried beans; cheese or fish on Thursdays, Sundays, and feast days; and whatever vegetable was in season. The vegetables were usually cooked in fat and seasoned with salt and pepper.

To see what vegetables were grown in the middle ages, a detailed list of plants provided by St. Hildegard of Bingen (1098-1179), most likely reflects what was grown in the gardens of her monastery. Many of them were known to the ancient Greeks and Romans: the broad bean (*Vicia faba*), cabbage and coleworts (*Brassica oleracea*), cucumber (*Cucumis sativus*), garlic (*Allium sativum*), leeks (*Allium porrum*), lettuce (*Lactuca sativa*), onions (*Allium cepa*), peas (*Pisumsativum*), radish (*Raphanus sativus*), shallots (*Allium ascalonicum*), and skirret (*Sium sisarum*). (It is worth noting here that some of the varieties we take for granted today, like Cos lettuce, originated on the Greek island of Kos; it is because it was so popular among the Romans that we also call it Romaine lettuce.) St. Hildegard also

lists artichokes (*Cynara scolymus*), carrots (*Daucus carota*), celandine (*Chelidonium majus*), celery (*Apium graveolens*), chickpeas (*Cicer arietinum*), cress (*Lepidium sativum*), dill (*Pencedanum graveolus*), sweet gale (*Myrica gale*), germander (*Teucrium chamaedrys*), gourd (*Lagenaria vulgaris*), lentils (*Lens esculenta Moench*), mustard (*Sinapis alba*), orach (*Atriplex hortensis*), origano [sic] (*Origanum vulgaris*), parsley (*Petroselinum crispum*), purslane (*Portulaca oleracea*), spurge (*Euphorbia spp.*), and watercress (*Rorippa nasturtium*). Her carrots were probably less full-bodied than the ones we are used to today, which are the result of French experiments in the second half of the nineteenth century. And of course many vegetables we take for granted were unknown in the Europe of St. Hildegard, including potatoes, tomatoes, corn, and squash.

Finally, a word about monastic contributions to the cultivation and study of edible plants. The Capuchin monks of Belgium have lent their names to at

S EXTENSIONS OF THE VEGETABLE GARDEN,

ORCHARDS AND VINEYARDS ARE LOCATED AT

THE LIMIT OF THE CLAUSTRAL RANGE, WHERE

THE DISTINCTION BETWEEN GARDENING AND FARMING DEPENDS PRINCI-

PALLY ON THE SCALE OF THE ENTERPRISE. HISTORICALLY, THE DILIGENCE

AND DISCIPLINE OF THE LAY BROTHERS WHO DID THE FARMING FOR THE

MONASTERIES GUARANTEED SUCCESS IN FRUIT GROWING AND VITICUL-

TURE. UNLIKE THE CHOIR MONKS, THESE PRACTICAL, HANDS-ON MEN

PRECEDING PAGES:
Beehives surrounded by apple trees at Saint Mary's Abbey, West Malling, Kent, England.

OPPOSITE:
Apple blossoms and wildflowers at Tymawr Convent, Gwent, Wales.

IT WAS FROM MONASTIC **EXPERTISE**

AND MAKING **WINE** THAT THE NATIONAL

had not taken vows to attend all the divine offices and so were free to take on the bulk of the field work, returning in the evening with red faces flushed by fresh air and soiled hands. Because of them, by the later Middle Ages monasteries had become leaders in reclaiming marshland and developing water control for irrigation, mills, and sewage. It was from monastic expertise in growing fruit, raising sheep, and making wine that the national economies of Europe later grew.

The principal products of monastic orchards and vineyards can be divided into three categories: Apples and cider; other fruits; and wine and liqueurs.

I. APPLES AND CIDER

It is easy to imagine how a monk pruning an apple tree might muse on the Bible and the symbolism of the apple, his memory perhaps refreshed by readings from the day's liturgy. He would think: "Here is a fruit of dubious distinction: in the hands of Christ, it symbolizes salvation, but in the hands of Adam it stands for evil." The connection between the apple and evil would be clear to him from the Latin words, which have the same form (*malum*). Although the Bible does not specify that the fruit of the tree of knowledge was an apple (and could not easily have been since apples are not

TOP:
Medlar fruit.

LEFT:
Windfall apples and pears.

ABOVE:
Plums on the tree.

N GROWING **FRUIT**, RAISING SHEEP,

ECONOMIES OF EUROPE LATER GREW.

TOP:
Quince on the tree.

RIGHT:
Plums.

ABOVE:
Kiwis on the tree.

native to the Middle East), our monk would know that it is usually depicted as an apple tree and might well question the propriety of cultivating a fruit that has such dark associations.

The orchard apple's derivation, which developed from wild crab apples crossbreeding and early man cultivating the larger fruits, goes back a very long time. They are mentioned in the earliest work of Western literature, Homer's *Odyssey* (ninth century B.C.), and the second-century B.C. Roman writer Marcus Portius Cato gives details of grafting and other aspects of apple husbandry. At the turn of the twelfth century, new strains of

apple that the French developed from dwarf stock were espaliered and trained to grow on trellises. Randomly pollinated cider apples were normally grown from seed, but the new dessert apples the French were anxious to develop required grafting, to maintain the parented qualities. By the end of that same century the Cistercians at Morimond, northeast of Langres, France, were sending apple grafts, seeds, and slips to the north and east of Germany. The English monasteries of Christ Church Canterbury and Bury St. Edmunds were known to have orchards at that time, as well.

Apples were eaten fresh, cooked, or

dried, and a mixture of cider and quince was boiled down to make apple butter. With hay, apples provided winter feed for livestock. As their cultivation spread in the Middle Ages, they became a valuable commodity. Wages, rent, and tithes could be paid in apples or in cider. They were stored in cellars in various ways—buried in fine white sand, piled and covered in straw, or packed into barrels with straw between the layers. Exceptionally fine apples were hung by strings from cellar beams to protect them from bruising. Also, at a time when people often got sick from drinking the water, fermented beverages—including apple cider—were known to be safe. Not only was apple cider safe, it was drunk as "wassail" for its beneficial qualities. Distilled cider or apple jack was as strong as brandy, had the same antiseptic properties, and was also good for preserving softer fruits like peaches, plums, and cherries. Finally, cider turned to vinegar was used to pickle vegetables and fruit.

Cider making began in September for a brew that could be drunk in March. It was labor intensive and required a good deal of skill. Local apples gave the ciders a distinctive taste and color, and they often had rich historical associations and colorful names, as can be judged from these examples from Devon and Somerset, England: Black Hereford, Chibble's Wilding, Hangdown, Kingston Black, Lurley Bittersweet, Cadbury, Tremlett's Bitter, Sweet Elford, Tom Putt, and Slack-my-girdle. The monks at Battle Abbey in Somerset still sell their surplus cider to the public.

Religious repression often spawned

OPPOSITE:
Espaliered apple trees behind the church at the Abbey of Fleury, Saint-Benoit-sur-Loire, France.

new churches in distant locations and with the communities came their horticultural techniques. The expulsion of the Huguenots from France by Louis IV, in 1685, for example, led to the introduction of apple growing and cider making techniques to the New World. Although the water was less polluted in America, the habit of drinking cider continued, due in no small part to its alcohol content.

Another fermented drink commonly made in monasteries was perry, from fermented pear juice. The pears were crushed and stored in wooden casks, and fermentation came from the natural yeast on the skin of the fruit. Slightly sweeter than cider, perry was a popular drink served with meals. Unfortunately, the number of varieties of pears and apples has fallen drastically in recent year throughout the world. For example, an Australian nursery, C. J. Goodman, offered 132 varieties of pears in 1911; in 1992 it offered only eight. This is typical of the standardization that has occurred throughout the

fruit growing industry with the result that most grocery stores only offer five varieties of pears: yellow and red Bartlett, green and red Anjou, and Bosc. The same is true of apples: there is on average a choice of perhaps five varieties that are released to the market from cold storage. Each of these commercial varieties looks and tastes the same in California, New York, France, and England. Take a Red Delicious standardized for the supermarket shelf: uniform in size and color, it tastes pre-dictably like a Red Delicious regardless of the season or the place. It is a known quantity holding no suprises, pleasant or unpleasant. Unfortunately, this massive commercialization produces an increasingly narrow gene pool and deprives us and our children of the taste of other kinds of apples, like the Baldwin, Black Oxford, Blue Pearman, Fameuse, Golden Russet, Grimes Golden, Hunt Russet, Maiden's Blush, or Coxe's Pippin, which are simply not available in stores.

Some monasteries, aware of the erosion in the gene pool, are growing apple varieties that are no longer in demand in order to protect them for the future. They also continue pruning apple trees in the traditional, visually appealing umbrella shape, even if this makes for a more difficult harvest than cordoned trees, which are pruned to grow at an angle. Monasteries know that these apples are not as commercially viable as the standardized varieties. As one of the nuns at West Malling, England, explains:

People expect perfect things all the time. When we pick our fruit we try to be careful but we don't have to be as careful as the commercial grower. If you have a blemish on an apple you cannot sell it. Well, we don't mind blemishes. I think that's important, really; you can have these apparently perfect apples, but what's gone into making them is something to think about.

Monasteries like West Malling are able to keep the old varieties going

because for them it is a spiritual enterprise and because they have a tradition of encouraging as much variety as possible within their walls. This is a reflection of the view that God's creation itself is infinitely various, like the individuals who make up the physical body of the Church. To limit variety is to go against the nature of what God provides us. How far will we have to travel down the road of uniformity before we realize what has been lost?

Most monasteries still have orchards, even if the trees are no longer pruned or cared for. Sometimes apple trees are tended for their ornamental value, as in the garden at Tymawr Convent in Wales. But orchards tend to survive even where vegetable gardens have been let go, and established trees are usually good for about fifty years. In those orchards that are active, the pruning and grafting continues now as it has for centuries past. The trees pass from one generation to the

next, offering up their fruit in harmony with the cycle of the liturgy and the seasons, new every year and as old as the monasteries themselves.

2. Other Fruits

Plums

When the monks of Solesmes bear flats of fresh-picked plums from the outer orchard to the kitchen, a spectacle of freshness passes by. The plums are different shapes and colors—red, purple, green, and yellow—and some are even bruised, but the skins still have the white sheen of yeast on them, smudged here and there by the hands that have picked them. The fruit's sweet smell wafts up from the flats. The monks' eyes are sparkling from the joy of the harvest. They will eat these plums after Vespers.

Medlars

The Medlar tree (*Mespibus germanica*) can live for three hundred years and is therefore often one of the oldest trees found in a monastery's orchard.

The medlar forms its fruit—a pome—from its bloom: it resembles a very small, compact apple which can be eaten fresh or made into jams and jellies. In the Middle Ages, in the form of ripe fruit or syrup, it was used to treat enteritis. The fruit is harvested following the first frosts, after bletting or softening and turning a rusty color.

Quince

Quince (*Cydonia oblonga*) are an ancient species originating in Asia and Mediterranean. The tree flowers early, heralding the arrival of spring. The fruit looks like a cross between and apple and a pear but has a distinctive flavor of its own; it turns green-yellow

OPPOSITE:
*Freshly picked plums
at Saint-Pierre Abbey,
Solesmes, France.*

when ripe. Quince are irregularly shaped and far from perfect; like the medlar, they have a medieval look. They stay hard and sour even when cooked, and since they have a high pectin level, they are ideal for making jam. There is a beautiful quince orchard at St.-George des Gardes which the nuns harvest for their trappist preserves.

MULBERRIES

The Book of Maccabbees, in the Apocrypha, tells how Judas Maccabaeus' soldiers crushed mulberries and grapes to make a blood-like liquid to incite elephants to battle (1 Maccabees 6:34). It is also said the murderers of Thomas Beckett met under a mulberry tree in Christ Church Canterbury to remove their coats. By the same token, the mulberry tree's blackish, blood-colored fruit symbolizes the passion of Christ.

Two species are commonly found in monasteries, as often in the ornamental garden as in the orchard. The leaves of the Mediterranean variety—*Morus*

LEFT:
A cherry tree in full bloom at the Little Portion Friary, New York.

alba—are the silk worm's favorite food, while the large dark fruit of *Morus nigra* can be eaten fresh or made into wine or jam. The mulberry's dark purple juice is used to add color and flavor to medicines even today.

CHERRIES

The cherry tree's beautiful bloom and distinctive bark make it a favorite nowadays for ornamental use, but it is the fruit which has been historically important for monasteries. The basic cornelian cherry (*Cornus mas*), which erupts into sprays of yellow flowers early in the spring, produces a red or yellow fruit resembling an elongated olive, while the sweet cherry (*Prunus avium*) is the stock for most modern hybrids.

For Christians, the cherry symbolizes the sweet character of the fruit of good works: in paintings when held in the fingers of the Christ child, it signifies the pleasures of the blessed. Both the cornelian and the mazzard are

asked him about this, Jesus took the opportunity to give them a lesson about the importance of absolute faith.

Figs have been grown in monasteries from the earliest times. There is nothing more delicious than the fresh fruit. Even in England, where they must be carefully protected from frost, espaliered fig trees bear good fruit on many a south-facing wall.

A photographer working in the garden at Sainte Scholastique Abbey was given a bag of refreshments by one of the nuns who had worked in the garden since entering the order. She set the bag on the ground and left him alone in this beautiful place that few outsiders had been privileged to see, let alone photograph. He became absorbed in his work. After a half-hour searching for the vantage point to best capture the essence of the garden, he set up his tripod—and discovered that this was exactly where the nun had left the bag. Inside it he found some juice, three fresh figs, and a lesson in humility.

RIGHT:
Beehives at Notre Dame des Gardes Abbey, St.-George des Gardes, France, where the nuns make their own honey.

alba—are the silk worm's favorite food, while the large dark fruit of *Morus nigra* can be eaten fresh or made into wine or jam. The mulberry's dark purple juice is used to add color and flavor to medicines even today.

CHERRIES

The cherry tree's beautiful bloom and distinctive bark make it a favorite nowadays for ornamental use, but it is the fruit which has been historically important for monasteries. The basic cornelian cherry (*Cornus mas*), which erupts into sprays of yellow flowers early in the spring, produces a red or yellow fruit resembling an elongated olive, while the sweet cherry (*Prunus avium*) is the stock for most modern hybrids.

For Christians, the cherry symbolizes the sweet character of the fruit of good works: in paintings when held in the fingers of the Christ child, it signifies the pleasures of the blessed. Both the cornelian and the mazzard are

mentioned as early as Charlemagne's *Capitulare*.

FIGS

In hot climates the fig tree (*Ficus carica*) is known for its fruit and the welcome shade it gives. It figures prominently in the Bible, beginning with the garden of Eden, where Adam and Eve, once they had lost their innocence and realized they were naked, sewed fig leaves together to cover themselves (Genesis 3:7). The Old Testament mentions pressed fig cakes as a source of nourishment for travelers (1 Samuel 25:18). In the New Testament a fig tree is famously singled out by Jesus. On his way to the Temple in Jerusalem, where he would overturn the moneychangers' tables and chase out the merchants, Jesus cursed a fig tree that was in leaf but bore no fruit, saying: "May no one eat of your fruit again!" The next day the tree was found to have withered to its roots (Mark 11: 12-20). When the amazed disciples

LEFT:
A monk holds freshly picked figs at Abbey of En Calcat, Dourgne, France.

3. Wine and Liqueurs

There is early mention of apples, pears, plums, medlars, mulberries, figs, quince, peaches, and cherries in both Charlemagne's *Capitulare* and St. Hildegard of Bingen's writings. There is, however, no fruit that is more central to Christian symbolism than the grape, along with the vine that bears it and the wine that is made from it.

On the evening before his death, Jesus Christ gave his disciples bread and wine as symbols of his body and blood, which he was about to sacrifice on the Cross—the act Christians believe fulfills God's covenant with mankind and illustrates His forgiveness of our sins. It is the very heart of Christianity. Christians commemorate the Sacrifice of the Cross in the Eucharist, a reenactment of the Last Supper that features the consumption of bread and wine. The ritual of holy communion is as old as Christianity, having been practiced initially in private homes and meeting rooms and later, after the legalization of Christianity by the Emperor Constantine in 312 A.D., in churches and monasteries. The Eucharist has a twofold spiritual significance: sacramental and also representative of Christ and the Trinity. In holy communion, the Christian believes he receives the body of Christ, and that the love of God in Christ is effective within him to the degree in which he believes.

Even before the Last Supper, the vine and its fruit figured prominently in Jesus' teachings and the Old Testament. It is significant that his first miracle, at Cana, was to turn water into wine, even though he seemed annoyed by his mother's request that

OPPOSITE:
Grapes on the vine at Saint-Pierre Abbey, Solesmes, France.

he make this a sign of who he was (John 2:1-10). The fragrant flowering blossoms of the vine are used as poetry of love (Song of Songs 2:13) and as a symbol of fertility (Song of Songs 7:12). Jesus used the allegory of the vineyard in the parable of the tenants (Mark 12:1-10) and in the parable of the workers in the vineyard (Matthew 20:1-16). In another parable (John 15:1-2), he compares himself to the vine:

I am the true vine, and my Father is the gardener. He cuts off every branch in me that bears no fruit, while every branch that does he prunes so that it will be even more fruitful.

Because the vine and the wine that is made from it were considered gifts of God, they were associated with peace and tranquility, and the destruction of the vineyard or its failure to produce grapes was taken as an omen of death and devastation. The Bible also stresses the coexistence of the good and the bad: the wood of the grapevine is useless and

only good for burning, and wine in excess leads to ruin.

Grapes were one of the fruits that the Desert Fathers dreamt of as a heavenly reward for their virtue. On earth, they were considered a great delicacy. The story is told of how Father Macarius, one of the disciples of St. Anthony, received a gift of fresh grapes. Though he relished them, he passed them on to a Brother who was ill. This Brother, too, denied himself the pleasure of the grapes, giving them to another, and so forth until they had made the round of the community and were offered to Macarius again. He thanked God for the fortitude of his fellow monks, and the grapes remained uneaten.

The history of viticulture reaches back to the Neolithic period in the Near East and Egypt (8500-4000 B.C.). The science of cultivating grapes and making wine flourished in the Nile

delta and Palestine around 2700 B.C., and the Romans later introduced it to Western Europe. During the centuries of barbarian domination, monasteries safeguarded the ancient knowledge and practice of winemaking. Up to the French Revolution, religious houses had the finest and most extensive vineyards in France. When it was sold in 1791, the Cistercian monastery of Citeaux owned 9,800 acres of agricultural land—much of it given over to vineyards that later spawned the Burgundy wines of Clos-Vougeot and Romanée. The abbey of Cluny also made exceptional wines. Even England had its hand at the art when beginning around 1200 a century

of milder climate prevailed, though at their height English wines were never produced on the scale of France, Italy, and Spain. Today, German and Austrian wines with the word *Mönch* (monk) in their names bear witness to this past. The same is true of French wines named *Moines* (monks), *Pères* or *Mères*. Even the American wine industry has monastic roots, in the vineyards planted by Spanish Franciscans in the Napa Valley. To this day there is a Napa wine called Christian Brothers.

Viticulture is an intricate business. It involves knowing how to graft plants

and choose the ideal time for harvest, how much watering is required and how much space to leave between the vines, how to ward off birds and fungus, and how to protect against frost. All of this creates an intimate bond between grower and vine that culminates in the hard work of the harvest season, which gives such tangible evidence of the miracles of this life. It is fitting that there be celebration of the harvest, like the feast of St. Martin of Tours on November 11, when the first wine of the year's harvest—the "St. Martin wine"—is drunk. In North America, the Pilgrim fathers included the first wine of the wild grape harvest in their first Thanksgiving.

The Benedictine abbey founded at Liguge around 360 A.D. by the hermit St. Martin remains a thriving community well known for its red wine. Other French monasteries that sell their wine are Rougan in the Languedoc and St. Etienne de Lugdares. Perhaps the best-known liqueur-producing monastery in the world is the Grande Chartreuse at Voirons, which in 1605 began making a green liqueur as part of the quest for an "elixir of long life." Currently the monks make three varieties: green, yellow, and raspberry. Each batch uses as many as 130 ingredients and takes four years to mature. The island

monastery of Lerins, south of Cannes, makes liqueurs called "La Lerina" and "La Senacole," and the trappist community of Aiguebelle produces a fine liqueur. Still other French monasteries, like Solesmes, grow grapes and make wine exclusively for their own consumption.

Bee keeping is often an integral part of vineyards and orchards, as the blos-

soms need to be pollinated to bear fruit. A number of monasteries have become expert in this art, especially the outstanding example of Buckfast Abbey on Dartmoor in Devon. Brother Adam of Buckfast is the author of *In Search of the Best Strains of Bees*. He has traveled throughout Western Europe and Asia studying bees and bee keeping, and he has developed his own honey processing plant. He also invented special hives

Beehives at
The Abbey of
Gethsemani,
Kentucky, where
the monks make
honey for themselves.

for the local bees, which collect pollen from the heather on nearby Dartmoor.

Honey has been used traditionally to make mead, an alcoholic beverage of fermented honey and water. Adding spices like ginger, cinnamon, clove, and rosemary to mead produces a drink called *metheglin*. Mead with apple juice is called *cyser*, and mead with fruit, *melomel*. The taste varies from sweet to dry, but these drinks are deceptively strong. The Vikings drank mead in preparation for their devastating raids on Britain in the eighth century, and it is still made at Lindisfarne on the Island of Farne off the Northumberland coast. Farne is also known as Holy Island for St. Aidan, an Irish monk and bishop who went there from Iona in 635 A.D. and used it as a base for his apostleship in Northumberland.

6

BURIAL

IN THE

GARDEN

VISITORS TO THE ABBEY OF EN CALCAT

FOLLOW A MONK DOWN AN ALLEY OF PLANE

TREES, WHERE HE TURNS OFF INTO AN AREA

ENCLOSED BY A LOW HEDGE. "LET ME INTRODUCE YOU TO SOME OF MY

FRIENDS," HE SAYS, GESTURING AT THE SIMPLE MARKERS. ALTHOUGH THE

STONES LIST ONLY NAMES AND DATES, THE MONK SPEAKS OF HIS

DEPARTED BROTHERS WITH SUCH PASSIONATE INTIMACY THAT THE

VISITOR FEELS THEY ARE VERY MUCH ALIVE. HE REALIZES THAT IN

DEATH THEY ARE AS MUCH AN INTEGRAL PART OF THEIR COMMUNITY

PRECEDING PAGES:
*Only red roses are planted
in the burial garden at
Notre Dame des Gardes
Abbey, St.-George des
Gardes, France.*

OPPOSITE:
*The old burial garden
at Stanbrook Abbey,
Worcester, England.*

FOR THE RELIGIOUS, **DEATH** IS LIKE MOVING INTO

WELL LIVED THAT LEADS TO ANOTHER LIFE

as they were when living, and that the place where they are buried is a place for the living to visit and reflect on the lives of those who went before them.

This tends to be a joyous meditation. As a nun at another monastery remarked after putting a fellow sister to rest, "Death is victory and triumph: it is graduation." For the religious, death is like moving into a new house: it is the triumph of a life well lived that leads to another life closer to God, a happy occasion—not an end but a transition. The funeral service, as monks have pointed out, is only of benefit to the living. Death does not need to be hidden away.

Like so many things in monastic life, this view reflects centuries of experience. Today, in secular society, death usually occurs far from the home, in

hospitals, under the auspices of the family but directly managed by doctors and nurses. It is often viewed as a frightening, embarrassing, and even shameful end, an obligation to be met with the unwritten protocol of "Let's just get through this as best we can." We tend to shield our children from death and even to deny full knowledge of what is happening to the dying person himself, in the belief that this will spare him pain. In the Middle Ages, individuals took charge of their deaths. They perceived no need to hide it away or sweep it under the carpet. On the contrary, the dying were encouraged to prepare themselves mentally and spiritually for death and to let others know what was expected of them. People preferred to die in their own bed, lying on their backs facing up to heaven, with

TOP:
*Burial cross at
Saint-Pierre Abbey,
Solesmes, France.*

LEFT:
*Burial cross at
Burford Priory,
Oxon, England.*

ABOVE:
*Crosses from
Holy Cross Abbey,
Virginia.*

A NEW HOUSE: IT IS THE **TRIUMPH** OF A LIFE CLOSER TO GOD, A **HAPPY OCCASION**...

TOP:
Burial cross at Abbey of Fleury, Saint-Benoit-sur-Loire, France.

RIGHT:
Crucified Christ at the head of the burial garden at Saint Mary's Abbey, West Malling, Kent, England.

family and friends all around, including children. Unlike modern hospitals, rooms for the dying were open to the world around.

Psychological preparation consisted of an interior process of grieving, of silently coming to grips with the sadness of leaving life and loved ones behind. When this was finished, the dying person addressed those gathered around the bed, forgiving them for any hurt they may have caused and asking their forgiveness in turn. Having dealt with the physical world, he would then turn his attention to God, making a public confession of his sins and praying to be granted entrance to paradise. When he felt death approaching, a priest offered absolution, sang psalms, and sprinkled holy water. Thus prepared, the person would remain in bed,

silently waiting to be taken. If death intervened on the road or in battle, the earth substituted for the bed. The dying faced Jerusalem and made the sign of the Cross over their chests or by fully extending their arms.

Those of us living in the secular world do not have to think about where on our property to bury our loved ones, unless perhaps they are pets. In a monastery it is a serious question. The solution is usually to mark off a space, still within the central area of the monastery for easy access to the living, with a low hedge or fence.

At Saint-Benoit-sur-Loire the remains of the founding St. Benedict are housed in a crypt beneath the altar of the church. In keeping with the

desire to be buried *ad sanctos*—that is, as close as possible to martyrs or saints—the monks' graves occupy a circular cemetery that hugs the curving outer walls of the basilica, just outside the choir. The crosses are uniform in size and shape and bear a small plaque with the monk's name and date of death (at some monasteries, like Solesmes, more than one monk is listed on each cross). At the Abbey of Bellefontaine in Begrolles-En-Mauges, France, the cemetery is in the middle of the main cloister at the very heart of the monastery, where it is seen by everyone in the course of their daily activities.

Not all monasteries follow this norm—some prefer to locate the cemetery in a place of exceptional natural beauty. Such is the case of Notre Dame Abbey in Le Bec Hellouin, France, where the burial ground overlooks a broad valley of shimmering poplars and grazing cows. It is located halfway between the abbey and the sister-convent of Sainte-Françoise Romaine. The nuns are buried there, too, on one side of a central granite

OPPOSITE:
The burial garden at St. Joseph's Abbey, Spencer, Massachusetts.

RIGHT:
The burial garden circles behind the crypt at the Abbey of Fleury, Saint-Benoit-sur-Loire, France, close to the remains of Saint Benedict.

cross representing Christ, with the monks on the other side. The crosses are uniform, to represent the equality of each person in the eyes of God. In its simplicity and dignity, this is a stunningly beautiful place.

Red roses and cyclamen were usually the only plantings in the cemeteries. The latter has a particular symbolism in Christianity, being known as "the bleeding nun" in memory of the Virgin Mary's sorrow, since there is a red spot in the center of the blossom, which droops like a

head bowed in grief. The red rose on the other hand is a symbol of martyrdom.

In the older of the two cemeteries at Stanbrook Abbey in England, which dates to the monastery's foundation in 1838, roses and old clematis climb the red brick walls of the enclosure while the borders feature peonies, irises, poppies, wallflowers, and red valerian. This is the burial place of nuns brought back from France in 1795. A neat and orderly modern cemetery is still in the making. The nuns are planting a shrub

LEFT:
The burial ground at the Abbey of Gethsemani, Kentucky, where writer Thomas Merton is buried.

garden there as a backdrop to a crucifix that the headstones face.

The cemetery at the Abbey of Gethsemani in Trappist, Kentucky, curves around a buttressed embankment overlooking a valley. Among the uniform white crosses lies the trappist monk and writer Thomas Merton. Merton died in bizarre circumstances while attending a Buddhist-Christian convention in Bangkok during Advent of 1968, apparently electrocuted by an electric fan. A great silence descended

on the monastery dining room after the evening meal that December 16 Abbot Flavin announced that Brother Thomas had died. Merton was a poet and autobiographer who also spoke out against the arms race and social injustice. He was a profound Christian and, although he questioned society both inside and outside of the monastery, Merton managed to keep his writing within the limitations set by the abbot. He had an unconventional life for a monk, and there are

still those who question whether his death was accidental.

One of the brothers who knew Merton when he was novice master speaks of him with deep respect. He remembers how during his period as a hermit, Merton asked him to celebrate Mass with him one day:

It was the most beautiful thing I've ever heard, though it was very simple. Merton knew the Latin very well; he knew the rhythm and beauty of the language, when all I *knew was the responses. There was no stopping him. It just kept coming out, and it was awesome.*

Regarding the untimely death, this monk wished that he could have had more time to learn from Merton but accepted his death:

It was time. The Lord just brought him in, and it was probably a good thing, as Merton is more popular now than ever before. Very few people are able to combine so many categories in one person;

*The burial garden at
Notre Dame Abbey,
Le Bec Hellouin, France,
overlooks the fertile
valley; monks and nuns
are laid to rest on either
side of the granite cross.*

*Merton managed it because every-
thing he did was centered in Christ.*
Even in burial he went against the
norm: monks are usually buried in
their habits, without a casket, but
Merton's body was so badly burned
that an exception had to be made.

The grounds of the cemetery at
Gethsemani curve along the top of a
buttressed embankment with a view of
a valley and the woodlands beyond.
Merton's cross is just like all the others,
but much of the grass is missing from

around it, as visitors like to take it for
mementos. The monk who had said
mass with Merton chuckles to think of
this "desecration": He often said,
"Well, when it's time for me to go—
when it's time for pushing up the
daisies—I won't be here anyway."
Monastic cemeteries are very much
alive for the members of the community, where the love and friendship that
grows up over years of working and
worshipping together continues to live
on, at the heart of the enclosure.

7

THE

GUEST

HOUSE

GARDEN

OSPITALITY IS ONE OF THE MONASTERY'S PRIMARY MISSIONS. AS ST. BENEDICT IN-STRUCTED: "ALL WHO ARRIVE AS GUESTS ARE TO BE WELCOMED LIKE CHRIST, FOR HE IS GOING TO SAY, 'I WAS A STRANGER AND YOU WELCOMED ME.'" THIS OPENNESS TO THE PUBLIC HAS NOT GONE UNNOTICED IN THE WORLD OUTSIDE THE MONASTERY WALLS, AND GUEST ROOMS MUST OFTEN BE BOOKED WELL IN ADVANCE. BUT MONASTERIES ARE NOT HOTELS: THEY ARE PLACES OF REFUGE, WHERE PEOPLE CAN WITHDRAW FROM THE BUSINESS OF THEIR DAILY LIFE.

PRECEDING PAGES
AND OPPOSITE:
*The guest house garden
at Tymawr Convent,
Gwent, Wales, includes
colorful borders and a
sunken Victorian garden.*

GUEST ACCOMMODATIONS ARE SĬMPLE AND QVĬEŤ

Some offer guided retreats over the course of a weekend, usually centered on a specific theme; others allow for unstructured personal retreats. Guest accommodations are simple and quiet—just enough space to breathe, rest, and meditate.

Although the gardens and guest accommodations are usually located on the monastery grounds with access to the chapel and perhaps the dining hall, the enclosure itself is normally closed to outsiders. Each monastery interprets differently St. Benedict's injunction to the monks against conversing with visitors without special authorization from the Abbot, but as a rule, members of the community do not mingle with visitors. The noteworthy exception to this rule is the nun or monk in charge of visitors, the Guest Mistress or Guest Master, who books rooms, takes guests in hand when they arrive, and relays special requests to the abbot or abbess.

People are drawn to monasteries for many reasons. Some are on a spiritual quest: they sense that they will find answers among these people who have had the courage to leave the secular world behind in order better to focus on the fundamental questions of life. As Brother Michael, the Guest Master at Solesmes, can attest, guests' questions often take shape clearly for the first time in the quiet of the guest house garden:

> Things happen for the guest in the garden. That is where they come to the realize that we have something here. They may not understand what it is, but they know there is something.

The guest garden at Solesmes is

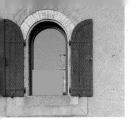

—JUST ENOUGH SPACE TO BREATHE, **REST,** AND MEDITATE.

divided into a variety of "rooms," each of which contains two or three sitting areas. Here the guest can find solitude for reading or sit conversing with others, it is also where guests meet with the monks for spiritual direction. There is a tiny pool in the middle, with running water, watched over by a statue of the Madonna and Child. Lantana are set in pots around the pool, and behind it pink roses cascade down a terrace wall. There is birdsong and the soft murmur of voices and the chiming of the chapel bells. At times sounds from the village float over the wall, or one hears a passing motorcycle or truck. It is like being on a boat that is pulling free of the harbor, leaving the busy world behind.

The guest house of the Tymawr Convent in Wales is in the remains of a Victorian garden. Once very densely planted, the garden proved too difficult to keep up and has since been substantially thinned, but it remains a magical place. All is green, with ferns and moss overflowing the wall of rough-cut granite stones that surrounds the sunken central area with its heart-shaped pool. Here there are purple granny's bonnets (*Aquilegia vulgaris*) and dark-yellow Welsh poppies (*Meconopsis cambrica*). Hidden amongst the ferns is a granite cross with a Celtic crucifix. As if to counterbalance this lush green place, the garden on the other side of the guest house is wildly colorful, a brash border of oriental poppies, cranesbill, lupines, pinks, wallflowers, lady's mantles, irises, and foxgloves.

The guest gardens of New World monasteries are no less beautiful.

Mepkin Abbey, located on the site of a former rice plantation beside the Cooper River near Charleston, South Carolina, is a fine example. The property had belonged to Henry and Clare Booth Luce, who commissioned the landscape architect Loutrel Briggs to create the gardens. Mrs. Luce, who admired Thomas Merton's writing, gave the property to the Bishop of Charleston and invited Gethsemani to found a new abbey there. The monks have diligently maintained the gardens for their own use and the enjoyment of their guests. Live oaks with drifts of hanging moss form the backdrop to the three-tiered formal garden of camellias and azaleas, with views of the slow-moving river where blue herons and alligators have lived for generations.

There are many forms of guest house gardens, but the essential ingredient is a place apart from the world where beauty, silence, and stillness reign. Many are perennial flower gardens, similar to small country house gardens.

OPPOSITE:
The guest house garden with mixed plantings at Saint-Pierre Abbey, Solesmes, France.

RIGHT:
The original guest house at Solesmes has grapevines growing on its walls.

Often these gardens are better planted and cared for than those inside the monastic enclosure. Regular guests sometimes want to give back a little of what they have received by volunteering to help in the garden, where there is always work to be done. Brother William of the Holy Cross Monastery in West Park, New York, happily reports that their guest house garden now has a special "lawyers' walk" after two lawyers volunteered to weed it.

There are indications that guest house gardens are a monastic tradition of long standing. Archaeological studies of Rievaulx, Kirkstall, Fountains Abbey, and Thornholme Priory in England have revealed that the guest houses of these monasteries were built soon after completion of the chapel, a good indication of their importance to the community in the days when ordinary travelers as well as pilgrims depended on monasteries to provide them a safe haven on their journeys. Stables were provided for horses, and

the wealthier monasteries offered different degrees of comfort in keeping with their visitors' social status. We do not know how common guest house gardens were in the Middle Ages, but those monasteries that had a separate garden for the abbot may well have opened it to the better-off guests. Such gardens, which as attachments to the abbot's semi-private quarters tended to be outside the community proper, are still in existence at La Neyte near Westminster Abbey and Silkstead of St. Swithun's Priory in England.

The existence of such privileges might seem to contradict the Benedictine injunction against the ownership of private property. The Rule specifies:

> *Whether monks may have personal property...It is of the greatest importance that this vice should be totally eradicated from the monastery. No one may take it upon himself to give or receive anything without the Abbot's permission, or to possess anything as his*

own, anything whatever, books or writing tablets or pens or anything at all; for they are not allowed to retain at their own disposition their own bodies or wills, but they must expect to receive all they need from the Father of the monastery.

We can only speculate that some abbots abused their power, knowing they exercised absolute authority over their fellow monks and believing they were answerable only to God.

Today few monasteries adhere strictly to the rule against personal possessions, but the ideal of removing material things from one's life so as better to focus on spirituality remains a foundation of monastic living. By leaving behind the telephone, the television, and the unpaid bills in order to sit on the garden bench and smell the roses, guests at monasteries are able, for a little while at least, to introduce this ideal into their own lives.

OPPOSITE:
Potted lantana surrounds a small pool at the guest garden at Saint-Pierre Abbey, Solesmes, France.

RIGHT:
A small, private prayer bench at Notre Dame Abbey, Le Bec Hellouin, France.

8

PLACES
TO
PRAY

I N THE DARKNESS FOLLOWING COMPLINE, A VISITOR TO THE GARDENS OF SAINT MARTIN ABBEY IN LIGUGE, FRANCE, MIGHT COME UPON A MONK IN PRAYER. HIS PROFILE OUTLINED BY LIGHT FROM A NEARBY HALLWAY, THE MONK SITS PERFECTLY STILL WITH HIS HOOD PULLED UP OVER HIS HEAD, DEEP IN PRAYER. THERE IS SOMETHING GHOSTLIKE ABOUT THE HALF-LIT FORM, AND THE VISITOR FEELS SLIGHTLY EMBAR-RASSED TO HAVE INTRUDED ON THIS INTENSELY PRIVATE MOMENT.

PRECEDING PAGES:
Monks return for Compline after walking in the French garden at Saint-Pierre Abbey, Solesmes, France.

OPPOSITE:
This prayer seat has a view of the Loire Valley at the Abbey of Fleury, Saint-Benoit-sur-Loire, France.

IN THE GARDENS, **PRAYER** IS GENERALLY

SITTING AREAS OR ALONG

This is what a relationship to God requires: quality time for intimate prayer, perhaps most of all for the members of monastic communities who live a life of constant worship and whose life's work is to be in prayerful dialogue with God. As mentioned before, prayer takes many forms in a monastery. It is present communally in the liturgical office, and in their daily work, but it also takes place in the privacy of cells and the sheltering spaces of fields and gardens. Religious often feel they don't spend enough time in solitude. Thomas Merton for one was frustrated by how little time his daily schedule of liturgy, serving as novice master, and writing left him for private communication with God. His frustration drove him to request permission to live apart from the other monks in a

hermitage on the grounds of Gethsemani, where he was finally able to spend some time in solitary prayer.

Today most monasteries recognize that their members require periods of escape from the pressures of life in their closely knit communities. There are two small chalets in the gardens of West Malling, for example, where nuns can "take a holiday" from their normal duties. Some monasteries park trailers in the woods for this purpose or erect small cabins like the retreat house at St.-George des Gardes. To be a permanent hermit on the monastery grounds is an unusual occurrence: one must be a member for several years (in some cases twenty-five) and receive the blessing of the abbot and the majority of one's fellow monks or nuns.

TOP:
A semicircular prayer bench at Saint Mary's Abbey, West Malling, Kent, England.

LEFT:
A prayer seat made from old column capitals at Saint Martin Abbey, Liguge, France.

CONDUCTED EITHER IN **SECLUDED**

THE **PA†HS** AND WALKWAYS.

ABOVE:
Benches arranged for corporate prayer at Abbey of Fleury, Saint-Benoit-sur-Loire, France.

RIGHT:
A wooden bench at Tymawr Convent, Gwent, Wales.

The everyday need for private prayer is often answered within the monastery's gardens. Some monks find that being outdoors brings them into contact with God's creation in a way that facilitates prayer. (This is not true for all: one nun who grew up in New York City searches out recesses hidden deep within the monastery buildings, where she feels safer and more at home.) In the gardens, prayer is generally conducted either in secluded sitting areas or along the paths and walkways. These places of prayer are the most utilized features of the garden by the community as a whole. Even the infirm are wheeled out into the garden to places where they can sit and pray in nature. Prayer is what sets apart a monastic garden from the secular.

The practice of walking in prayer is very old. The body's movement helps to still the mind and center oneself for a conversation with God. Monks walk in prayer extensively and design their gardens to have walkways of different lengths and moods.

In medieval times, the concept of going on a journey to commune with God was practiced by pilgrimages to holy places and crusades to Jerusalem. Pilgrims to Santiago de Compostela in northwestern Spain, the acclaimed burial spot of St. James the Apostle, created a support system of monasteries and churches stretching across France and Spain along the pilgrims' way. The crusaders to the Holy Land also felt that their journey was a necessary part of their spiritual life to bring them closer to God.

When the last of the Crusades was over, many of the gothic cathedrals, including Chartres, Amiens, and Rheims, built stone labyrinths on the floor of the nave. They became a symbolic alternative to the crusades and Christians could undergo a journey to commune with God by walking them. The labyrinths are divided into three stages: the first, leading toward the center, stands for release from the stressful burdens of everyday life; the second, standing in the center, represents restful repose in prayer and opening ourselves to the light of God; the third is the return journey where we return to our lives in the world joined with God. The faithful pray for guidance at the outset of the walk and meditate on the request throughout the journey. Additional symbolism depends on the individual labyrinth. At Chartres, for example, the six-petalled rose in the center symbolizes the kingdoms of creation: mineral, plant, animal, human, angelic, and the unknown. A contemporary revival of interest in walking prayer accounts for the labyrinth and prayer garden that the Community of the Holy Spirit in Brewster, New York, has built on the site of a former swimming pool.

Other monasteries simply provide paths for their members. In the formal garden at Solesmes, there is something almost regal about the sight of the strolling monks in their black habits.

This is a sunken garden with a central walkway punctuated by topiary balls, cubes, and cones of yew and lateral alleys of trees that soar like the columns of a gothic cathedral. Walking the side alleys is like walking around the gallery of a cloister garth, except that this garden offers the option of sunlight or shade, long walks or short ones.

There are many variations on the theme. The prayer walk of the Abbey of Bellefontaine goes along the edge of a field and the shore of a lake, while the paths at Downside in England make their way beneath a canopy of mature trees before plunging into woods. At West Malling the paths have perennial borders, and at Tymawr they cut

ABOVE:
A corridor of trees forms a walkway for prayer at the Abbey of En Calcat, Dourgne, France.

through fields of wild flowers. The Convent of the Incarnation in Fairacres, England, offers yet another variation. Located in the city of Oxford, the convent is surrounded on three sides by terraced housing. The nuns have accordingly planted a small woodland on the property with different varieties of trees and a path running through the middle.

Praying in a garden or simply outside in any natural spot can enhance one's private relationship with God. We know Jesus Christ liked to pray in nature. The gospel of Luke outlines how Christ always prayed at important times in his life: at his baptism (3:21),

before choosing the apostles (6:12), at the Transfiguration (9:29), prior to his betrayal (22:39-46), and his crucifixion (23:46). His habit of praying in the garden at Gethsemane enabled Judas to lead the chief priests and Pharisees to arrest him.

The significance of Jesus' model of prayer to the disciples and ultimately to Christians today, was to show them how to have an intimate relationship with God. Jesus knew very well that prayer was the key to his relationship with the Father, as his own prayer—the Lord's Prayer—makes clear (Luke 11:2-4). The essence of his teaching was to communicate this simple but overwhelmingly important fact to his disciples, and through them to all the faithful down through the ages. Since prayer in its many aspects is the very core of monastic life, intimately bound up with the rhythms of the liturgical cycle and the four seasons, these communities must provide surroundings that are conducive to the silent withdrawal from other cares that is the prelude and context of private prayer. The gardens we have been examining are thus directly connected with the living God and the teachings of his Son; they have been a part of monastic life from their foundation nearly seventeen hundred years ago to the present.

Adels, Jill Haak. *The Wisdom of the Saints*. New York: Oxford University Press, 1987.

Aries, Philippe. *Western Attitudes Towards Death: From the Middle Ages to the Present.* Baltimore: The Johns Hopkins University Press, 1974.

Braunfels, Wolfgang. *Monasteries of Western Europe: The Architecture of the Orders.* London: Thames and Hudson, 1972.

Cary-Elwes, Columba, O.S.B. *Monastic Renewal.* New York: Herder and Herder, 1967.

Cogliati Arano, Luisa. *The Medieval Health Handbook: Tacuinum Sanitatis.* New York: George Braziller, 1976.

Coppack, Glyn. *English Heritage Book of Abbeys and Priories.* London: B.T. Batsford/English Heritage, 1990.

Edwards, Tudor. *Worlds Apart: A Journey to the Great Living Monastaries [sic] of Europe.* New York: Coward-McCann, 1958.

Ferguson, George. *Signs & Symbols in Christian Art.* New York: Oxford University Press, 1954.

Hamilton, Geoff. *The Organic Garden Book.* London: Dorling Kindersley, 1987.

Harvey, John. *Mediaeval Gardens.* London: B.T. Batsford, 1981.

Kline, Francis, O.C.S.O. *Lovers of the Place: Monasticism Loose in the Church.* Minnesota: Liturgical Press, 1997.

Landsberg, Sylvia. *The Medieval Garden.* New York: Thames and Hudson, 1996.

McIntyre, Anne. *The Medicinal Garden: How to Grow and Use Your Own Medicinal Herbs.* New York: Henry Holt and Co., 1997.

McNamara, Jo Ann Kay. *Sisters in Arms: Catholic Nuns Through Two Millennia.* Cambridge: Harvard University Press, 1996.

Merton, Thomas. *No Man is an Island*. New York: Harcourt, Brace and Co., 1955.

Oakley, Anne M. *Malling Abbey: A History to Celebrate, Nine Hundred Years, 1090-1990.* Malling Abbey, 1990.

OPPOSITE:
Paths lead to a prayer bench in the wildflower garden at Tymawr Convent, Gwent, Wales.

Parry O.S.B., Abbot, and Esther de Waal. *The Rule of Saint Benedict*. Leominster: Gracewing Books, 1990.

Payne, Raef and Wilfrid Blunt. *Hortulus by Walafrid Strabo*. Pittsburgh: Hunt Botanical Library, 1966.

Peplow, Elizabeth and Reginald. *In a Monastery Garden*. Newton Abbot: David and Charles Inc., 1988.

Sanecki, Kay N. *History of the English Herb Garden*. London: Ward Lock, 1992.

Seward, Desmond. *Monks and Wine*. London: Mitchell Beazley, 1979.

Sitwell, Sacheverell. *Monks, Nuns, and Monasteries*. New York: Holt, Rinehart, and Winston, 1965.

Taylor, Norman. *Taylor's Guide to Vegetables and Herbs*. New York: Houghton Mifflin, 1987.

Ward, Benedicta, S.L.G. *The Lives of the Desert Fathers*. Russell Norman trans. Michigan and Oxford: Cistercian Publications and A.R. Mowbray, 1981.

Watson, Benjamin, ed. *Taylor's Guide to Heirloom Vegetables*. New York: Houghton Mifflin, 1996.

Weiser, Francis X. *Handbook of Christian Feasts and Customs*. New York: Harcourt, Brace and World, Inc., 1958.

Wynne, Peter. *Apples*. New York: Hawthorne Books, 1975.

INDEX

(Page numbers in *italic* refer to illustrations.)

DESIGNER: Nina Barnett
PROJECT EDITOR: Julie Ho
PRODUCTION: Kim Tyner

The text of this book
is composed in Granjon

Printed and bound in Great Britain
by Butler & Tanner Ltd.